Can't you control your child?

The true story of a father and his ADHD son

R. A. Collins

Published by R A Collins, Ipswich

Also by R. A. Collins

Treasure This Day (2006) Martal Publications of Ipswich, Ipswich, ISBN 1-90325-634-8; paperback; 56 p., ill. (some colour), 21 cm; cancer – patients – family relationships, cancer – patients – biography

A Father's True Story of his ADHD Son (2006) Martal Publications of Ipswich, Ipswich, ISBN (10) 1-90325-632-1, ISBN (13) 978-1-9032563-2-9; paperback; 32 p., 21 cm; parents of children with disabilities – biography

Reflect on Sorrow: Two Families, Two Stories (2007) R A Collins, Ipswich, ISBN (10) 0-95548-360-3, ISBN (13) 978-0-9554836-0-8; paperback; v, 196 p., 20 cm; attention-deficit hyperactivity disorder – family relationships, developmentally disabled children – family relationships, cancer – patients – family relationships

ADHD: The Devil Within (2007) R A Collins, Ipswich, ISBN (10) 0-95548-361-1, ISBN (13) 978-0-9554836-1-5; paperback; 107p., 20 cm; attention-deficit hyperactivity disorder

The ADHD Interviews (2008) R A Collins, Ipswich, ISBN (10) 0-9554836-2-X, ISBN (13) 978-0-9554836-2-2; paperback; 100 p.; attention-deficit hyperactivity disorder, parents of children with disabilities – biography

NLA 5/10

First published by R A Collins, Ipswich, 2007

Revised edition of *ADHD: The Devil Within*

Published by R A Collins, Ipswich

Copyright © R. A. Collins 2007, 2009

A CIP catalogue record for this book is available from the British Library

ISBN (10) 0-9554836-3-8

ISBN (13) 978-0-9554836-3-9

Printed and bound in Great Britain by Copytech (UK) Limited (Printondemand-worldwide), 9 Culley Court, Bakewell Road, Orton Southgate, Peterborough, PE2 6XD

Editorial services provided by K Yarwood

8100490139

Contents

That being said, I hope that this book above all offers encouragement and inspiration, such as when you read of Daniel's astonishing achievements, which are proudly recorded herein. For us, though on many occasions things seemed utterly hopeless, there appeared in these accomplishments to be an increasingly brighter light to be glimpsed at the end of a very long and tortuous tunnel.

R. A. Collins, Ipswich, 2009

1 'Your baby is not behaving like a normal baby'

I am now 58 years of age and, although not quite in my 'senior years', I nonetheless find it really quite shocking when I think of how time has overtaken me. Reflecting back over years gone by, I am at times overwhelmed with sadness; an indescribable sadness, specifically concerning our son Daniel who, when first delivered to this world, suffered from asphyxia. That birth trauma has had a devastating effect many years on in the lives of everyone in my family – including Daniel, of course – and it seems simply impossible to imagine that it first came about more than 21 years ago. To me, it seems just like yesterday, so vivid are the memories.

It all began on Tuesday, 20 October 1987, when Daniel came into this world after my wife Rosemary's very long and distressing labour. He was very quickly surrounded by a team of doctors and nurses, who immediately began clearing his obstructed airways and commenced resuscitation. There was no crying from Daniel, no bellowing out as you would expect from a newborn child, just a lifeless bluish-coloured baby and a blanket of deathly stillness as the team fought on and on to save our son. Attempts at cardiac massage were persistently applied, the only signs of life in a concentrated silence.

Then, after approximately four long minutes of continuous resuscitation attempts and with the assistance of oxygen, Daniel slowly began to breathe; shallow, irregular breathing at first, but soon followed by a more stable pattern of inhaling and exhaling. His skin colour gradually improved, too, from the distressing blue tinge to a healthy-looking pink. My wife and I sighed with relief as we allowed our fears for our son to turn into at least a partial joy: we were only too aware that he was not out of the woods yet, but that this was undoubtedly a better starting point.

As soon as Daniel's breathing had stabilised to a level that was as good as could have been expected, considering the circumstances, he was quickly ushered away to the special care baby unit (SCBU) to be further assisted in his battle for life. Although we had been told that his condition had been stabilised, we were still obviously very anxious. After some further time had passed, my wife and I became increasingly worried, especially as we had not been given the opportunity to accompany our son to the intensive care unit, and so we had no option but to rely on the medical team to keep us informed regarding his condition.

It was later on in the morning, after more than two very long hours of waiting, that a female doctor approached my wife's hospital bed and explained to her in a matter-of-fact way: 'Your baby is not behaving like a normal baby.'

'What do you mean "not behaving like a normal baby"?' I asked.

'Well, the baby has suffered from a series of epileptic fits, which were very concerning. In fact, he required urgent medical intervention,' she replied. 'He has come through this OK, but I must tell you both that the baby's kidneys are not working, and we have started him on medication therapy to assist his kidneys with the outward flow of urine. We are also in the process of carrying out blood tests to establish what exactly is going on. We will need to perform a lumber puncture, too. Have you any questions?'

'Yes. What is a lumber puncture?' I asked, as I had no idea what this was or what the procedure entailed. In fact, I felt a little ignorant not knowing what this was at the time, although obviously I understand what the procedure is today.

The doctor replied: 'Well, we will insert a hollow needle into the baby's lower back region and withdraw cerebrospinal fluid, which we can then send to the lab for examination.'

'OK, doctor,' I said, 'But what are you hoping to find in the fluids?'

'We think that your son may possibly have a serious blood disorder called "septicaemia",' she said, before adding, 'We will know much more once all the tests are completed and the results are returned back from the laboratories.'

⌒⌒

After a few more hours had passed, and the doctors' efforts appeared to have resulted in Daniel being in a much more stabilised condition, we were allowed to visit him in the SCBU. We were not, however, able to hold or touch him because his immune system was virtually non-existent, and so any infections he acquired could be potentially life threatening. Just as we began to be assured that our son's condition was improving, though, things took another turn for the worse. As we watched a doctor attempting to fit a catheter into our baby's bladder to further assist him with his non-existent urine output, we noticed Daniel's skin colour suddenly change again from a healthy pink to that terrible blue, the awful pallor from his birth, and once again our joy turned to serious concern as the machines bleeped and, in a matter of seconds, his incubator was surrounded once again by a team of doctors and nurses. Our infant son was now fighting his second major battle – 'the battle to survive', yet again. Tears welled in my wife's eyes as her desperate screams brought comforting nurses to her aid.

Unable to assist in any practical way, and so feeling quite helpless, we could only stay out of the way and leave it all up to the doctors and nurses, each of whom appeared to be concentrating on their own specific tasks.

'Come on,' I thought. 'Breathe, please breathe.' I was also thinking, 'This is it,' and had almost begun to accept that Daniel was not going to pull through this episode. But, just then, as a doctor was administering oxygen into his tiny lungs and another was continuing with heart massage, we suddenly heard our son screaming at the top of his voice! As before, it seemed to us that the medical team must have been working on him for ages, but in reality it had obviously only been a few short moments. We both once more breathed sighs of relief and allowed ourselves to relax into a more joyful state, as once again our 'battler' boy returned to the land of the living, and the angels abated into the background and it seemed our prayers to God had once again been answered.

In fact, every time that things appeared to be going well and we picked ourselves up into more of a relaxed state, something would happen that would knock us down again. This time would be no different. The following day, my wife and I were approached by a senior doctor. 'The results from the lumber puncture have now arrived back from the laboratory', he announced sombrely, 'and I am sorry to tell you that your son is extremely ill.'

'He has septicaemia,' the doctor continued, 'and many of his vital organs are slowly shutting down one by one. He is completely overwhelmed by the disease and almost every organ in his body is affected. We have now started him on very high-dose antibiotic therapy, but I must stress to you again that he is extremely ill.'

'So, what are his chances?' I asked.

'It's very difficult to say,' replied the doctor. 'It actually all depends on how effective the antibiotics are going to be in fighting the disease, but I must advise you to be prepared for a worst-case scenario. Nevertheless, we are giving it our best shot and he has a fighting chance.'

My wife and I kept up our bedside vigil as the antibiotics were introduced intravenously into our tiny son's frail body. There were many catheters leaving Daniel's tiny body and each was performing its own particular task: one was relieving obstruction to his kidneys, accessing them through his urethra; another was feeding the high-dose antibiotics to all the organs throughout his body, slowly seeking out and destroying the bacteria that was extremely hostile, and which was attempting to end his life; further catheters and electrodes functioned to assist in the supporting of his life – and so all were as equally as important.

Each day that passed with our son surviving was indeed a blessing; in fact, each hour that passed was a blessing – and not only was it a blessing, but it was adding significantly to his chances of long-term survival.

We also knew, of course, that circumstances could change with the blink of an eye at any time.

The drug phenobarbitone that was entering our son's frail body through one of the catheters was doing its work and the epileptic seizures were being held at bay, at least for the time being. Whether or not this was going to continue no-one could predict, of course, and so, again, we were back to just waiting and watching. Further blood tests were taken a few days later, and we were overjoyed when it was confirmed that the antibiotics, too, appeared to be working; the septicaemia was also being defeated, albeit slowly; each organ affected by this mass poisoning was now slowly beginning to recover; the mannitol drug given for the renal problems had also started to get to work; and the urine had begun to flow, although only in tiny quantities, at first, but the output was increasing day by day. All in all, it was now looking like a case of 'onwards and upwards'.

Daniel's brain, too, was monitored on a fairly regular basis. I found it difficult to understand the meaning of these scans when the doctors spoke of 'high peaks more marked on one side than the other'. I was not a brain surgeon but merely a father, and so for the specialists to explain the scan results in such unfamiliar terms seemed really quite futile. (I did quickly learn the basics, such as, for example, the fact that the brain is divided into two halves and that the left side of the brain is responsible for functions on the right side of the body, while the right side of the brain is responsible for tasks on the left side of the body; so, at least I gained some understanding through the process, although I couldn't really imagine that this snippet of knowledge was really going to be of any great benefit to me in the long term – well, at least I didn't think so!).

With each day that passed, Daniel continued to show small improvements – which, of course, were huge improvements in the context of the critical condition from which he was now emerging. Those waiting angels, hovering for so long in the background, seemed slowly to be disappearing for good now as our tiny battler continued his fight to survive. It really was quite remarkable how he had overcome so many difficulties to survive to the stage he had reached at this point in time, and each day that followed we watched in the SCBU as our son's improvements continued. One by one, the catheters that had been in his tiny body were removed: first, the one that had been addressing his renal problems was removed; this was followed by the one that had been administering the antibiotics; next were the wires that had been closely monitoring his heartbeat and blood pressure.

Confident that the worst was surely almost over, we began to look forward to our son being discharged for a journey to a place where he belonged, a place where he should have been weeks earlier: our home. The doctor gave us a cocktail of drugs that we would need to give Daniel on a daily basis, including the phenobarbitone to

Preface

This book presents a candid account of my family's struggle raising our son Daniel, who, at birth, suffered from oxygen starvation to one of the most important organs in the human body: his brain. We believe that this early trauma led to the attention deficit hyperactivity disorder (ADHD) with which Daniel would later be diagnosed. It also seems likely that the oxygen deprivation at birth caused, or at least contributed to, Daniel's subsequent developmental disorders, learning difficulties, presentation of challenging behaviours, and, ultimately, autism.

In the text that follows, you will read of our son's harrowing delivery and of the medical negligence claim that followed; you will learn of his early fight to survive in the face of unrelenting obstacles, including septicaemia, epileptic seizures, and renal damage; you will consider, as we did, the potential value of alternative treatments, such as faith healing, homeopathy, and traditional Chinese medicine. Moreover, our story offers a first-hand evaluation of the educational opportunities available to someone like Daniel, which at times were frustratingly limited. It also lays bare his extreme behaviours and the effect that these had on our family as a whole.

ensure that the epileptic fits would not return. Walking across the hospital car park to fetch our car in preparation is a time that I will always remember: I recalled then that I had, in the first few days following Daniel's birth, thought to myself that this moment would never be, that our son was not going to survive. And while my thoughts had on occasion been really quite negative during this period, I had never dared once let on to my wife, instead accommodating the sad thoughts as 'just in case' feelings, and allowing that, if Daniel survived, as he eventually did, it would be a real bonus – which was now, as I walked back into the hospital, how it had turned out to be, thankfully. Driving home with our baby son made me feel really strange in a peculiar sort of way. It was somehow sorrow and elation combined into one: joy that he was finally coming home, yet a sadness for the insults to which his brain had been subjected, and anguish that he had been born in such a poor physical condition.

2 The 'waiting game'

It felt really good for us all to be together as a family unit, and it looked at that time very much as if things were going to turn out on a positive note. Perhaps, just perhaps, Daniel was not going to suffer from any long-term complications and, just maybe, the initial problems at his birth were going to finish there? Or, at least, this was what we were hoping for.

Our local general practitioner (GP) visited Daniel each day for the first two weeks after we came home from the hospital, just to keep an eye on his progress. Soon, the daily visits became weekly ones, and then monthly, and so on. Regular visits to our local hospital's Out Patients' Paediatric Department with Daniel became commonplace, along with regular brain scans and other medical procedures, and it was on one of these visits that I felt without doubt that I needed to ask the paediatrician what I considered to be an important and as yet unaddressed question: 'Do you know if this oxygen starvation that our son suffered from at birth going to affect him, and, if so, in what way?'.

'It's still fairly uncertain at the moment, Mr Collins,' the doctor replied. 'It may be that he is left with some quite minor problems, or it could be that he will be affected by much more significant problems. I am afraid it's just going to be a waiting game, and, as your son gets older, we will have a much clearer picture of any effects, mainly because we will be better able to observe his behaviours, amongst other things, better than we can in a newborn baby.'

'So, is there a chance he could be severely brain damaged?' I continued.

'Yes,' replied the doctor, 'But, as I explained, only time will tell – although I would like to say that if he escapes with no underlying problems whatsoever he will be very lucky indeed, considering the amount of time that had elapsed before he was able to breathe unaided. He was actually starved of oxygen for approximately four minutes and, in most cases where a baby has been deprived of oxygen for this amount of time, there are normally effects of some description.'

Afterwards, my wife and I could not get this possibility out of our minds: Daniel might be severely brain damaged and, while we knew this would be the worst-case scenario, we had to understand that it was a very real prospect. 'What would his quality of life be like if this were the case?' I thought to myself, and then once again all the negative thoughts returned to my mind: 'Would I want to live if I were severely brain damaged?' I wondered. 'No, I do not think I would,' I decided, while also recognising that this was only my conclusion, and that, after all, Daniel had the right to live whatever the outcome, and he deserved all the love and care we could give to him – and that positive thoughts always return to cloud over the negative ones.

Meanwhile, Daniel appeared to be making good, steady progress. There were no more epileptic fits – which was, at that particular time, one of our biggest concerns – but was it only the phenobarbitone medication that was preventing the fits from returning? In fact, we would very soon be in quite a good position to find out, as, after a few more months had passed, the paediatrician explained to us, during one of the regular hospital appointments, that he would like to try and wean Daniel off the phenobarbitone – but as a very gradual process. At first, our concerns grew as the doctor stressed to us that there was a possibility our son may suffer a relapse and experience more epileptic fits, which could possibly be a very serious situation, even life threatening, but that the only real way to find out whether or not he still required the drug was to withdraw it. And so the decision was made and the process of withdrawing the drug began. The first day with Daniel on the reduced dosage passed by slowly, as we watched and observed intently, hoping that all was going to be fine. By the end of that first day, everything was indeed fine; the second day was similar, and then the third, fourth, fifth, six, seventh... all went by without any apparent problems.

Two weeks passed, then a further reduction in the dosage was applied, and still everything appeared to be going well. As days turned into weeks, and weeks turned into months, we felt confident that Daniel had overcome another one of the major hurdles in his life; the epileptic seizures, and the drugs to control them, were no more. No longer facing a lifetime of suffering from epilepsy, we felt that this was indeed another fantastic step forward; our young son had cleared hurdles in a way that we never would have imagined possible in a million years. He was, in our eyes and without any doubt, a true battler, and for fighting so hard he really deserved to come through it all unscathed.

Life at home with our new baby son seemed set to stabilise into a happy, 'normal' rhythm. We did notice that, even as a young baby, he did not sleep as well as we might have expected, but we were not unduly concerned about this at the time. After a few more months had passed, however, we noticed something else that gave us more cause for concern, and while others might have considered it only a minor issue in isolation, to my wife and I, it seemed significant: we noticed that Daniel's head was constantly tilted to one side and rested on his shoulder. He was unable to support his head, even for short periods of time, and it was almost as if he had a broken neck. The only way that he could maintain his head up in an upright position was if my wife or I lifted it into an upright position and held it in place; should we have let go, his head would have simply dropped down and back onto his shoulder or chest. This, we quickly realised, should not really be happening in a young child. We knew that, at this stage in his development, he should have a certain degree of head control, even if it meant just holding his head up for a couple of minutes, but he had none whatsoever. We decided to make an appointment for Daniel to visit our family doctor at that time, who, after examining him, referred him to our local hospital's consultant paediatrician.

At the hospital, the paediatrician carefully examined Daniel, but did not appear to be overly concerned. Indeed, he said that the problem would probably correct itself as Daniel became a little older. But, for my wife and I, it was still concerning. We felt certain that this was not within the 'norm' expected from a child of Daniel's age. In fact, I had a gut feeling that this lack of head control was a consequence of our son's traumatic delivery; that it was part of some neurological disturbance connected to that incident.

Another potential issue was that Daniel was a very difficult baby to feed. Each feed took a huge amount of time, much longer than you might expect had your child been born without medical complications. In fact, each feed took so long that we took turns in feeding him, and by this I mean took turns during each feed. Normally, halfway through the bottle, I would take over from my wife, and vice versa, such was the amount of time it actually took for Daniel to finish his feed.

There was quite a large number of people, mostly professionals in one capacity or another, that came to visit Daniel in our home on a weekly basis, including health workers, social workers, and portage workers, to name but a few. Hardly a day would pass without such visitors calling by, and, on the days that there were none, we would be otherwise occupied with taking Daniel to the hospital, or some other venue to do with his wellbeing. There were actually very few days where we just had time to ourselves, and our family's everyday lives began to change so much – even at this early stage in Daniel's life. His older brother must have wondered why all these people came to visit Daniel yet nobody came to see him, and although we tried to explain, as best we could, why his brother was the focus of all this attention, we were never really sure that he understood. He seemed only to look at us in a way that was really very sad, and I just wished that I could have helped him realise what was going on, but, given that he was a relatively young child himself, I suppose that was a near impossibility.

The next few months quickly passed by and the time soon came when we really started to notice how Daniel seemed more and more to be exhibiting after effects of the birth asphyxia. Although we had observed things earlier, such as his poor head control and his profuse dribbling, it was not until he was aged around two years that he really started to show signs of having some neurological problems, and we were able to detect with certainty that things were not as they should have been. Daniel's extreme hyperactivity, for example, was simply unimaginable: it was almost as though he was possessed by some supernatural powers, and the hyperactivity was made much worse by his strength, which was absolutely unbelievable. Never before in my life had I witnessed a young child with so much strength. To move furniture from one side of the room to the other was an easy task for him, and it did not seem to matter to him how heavy the item of furniture was: if it was in the room, then he could move it.

By this stage, we were finding it increasingly difficult to cope on a day-to-day basis. For Daniel, remaining still was a no-go area, with even a couple of minutes of sitting still clearly a very difficult task for him to complete. We tried lots of different things to help him burn off his excess energy, but it was always my wife and I who were tired out while Daniel still had plenty of go left in him! Huge amounts of exercise and long walks did no good, and, even when we had finished a long walk, it was not unusual for me to then have to chase him after he would scarper away to somewhere that he was not supposed to go to. It was simply constant and unrelenting. We were offered plenty of advice from lots of people, including health professionals, on how to keep him focused, but nothing worked. Whatever we tried, even ignoring the bad behaviours and rewarding the good behaviours, was a complete waste of time, and simply did not work.

In many ways, I found it very sad, too, that Daniel was unable to remain still. After all, it was obviously way beyond his control. My instincts told me that our son needed a complete medical evaluation to get to the bottom of it all, and so I voiced our family's concerns many times to several of the organisations involved in our family difficulties at that time, but it all appeared to be leading nowhere. The time was fast approaching when we urgently needed some form of respite, even if just for a couple of hours, as we were now reaching our wits' end. However, there would be no respite support made available to us at that time, mainly because Daniel had been given no firm diagnosis.

We undoubtedly needed him to be diagnosed, not only to help us with respite care, but to enable us to seek out the best treatment options for him. We were advised by some people that we simply needed to 'be firmer with him', despite the fact that we had already been down that route and it patently did not work. It went much deeper than that, and I had a very good idea that our son was suffering from one form of neurological disorder or another; the one thing that really took over my mind was that he was suffering from a condition called 'ADHD' ('attention-deficit hyperactivity disorder' in full). It was these hunches that prompted me to find out more about the condition; in fact, it became my main objective in life, and nothing else seemed to matter, and so the search began.

I visited libraries, which I had never previously done in my life, I purchased a computer and slowly learned how to use it (and as many of the older readers will appreciate, we never had computers in schools in days gone by, so I became what you could describe as a 'mature student'). I observed two other children whom I knew were affected by the condition. I read books that were written by people who suffered from the disorder, in particular one detailing the life story of Ben Pollis, who was expelled from almost every school he went to, and whose life was very troubled by his ADHD condition, leading him into many conflicts with both those who loved him and the authorities. Ben's life turned for the better as he aged, though, and he now lectures at universities on the subject of ADHD. Perhaps understandably, I found this particular book very touching. I also read many other books on ADHD that explained the symptoms, treatments, and so on, and in doing so I became more convinced than ever that this disorder was affecting our son. I also knew instinctively that the ADHD was not Daniel's only problem, and that something else was in co-existence with this, my primary suspicion of ADHD, but felt that if at least the ADHD were diagnosed, then it would certainly be a good foundation indeed from which to pursue other evaluations at a later date.

Armed with my new learned knowledge of the ADHD disorder, I decided to consult again with the paediatrician about my concerns, explaining with no 'ifs' or 'buts' that I felt absolutely certain that our son was suffering from attention-deficit hyperactivity disorder. And, following another, thorough evaluation by doctor [X], the paediatrician, and a referral to a child psychiatrist, a diagnosis of ADHD was finally given. At last: a firm diagnosis. It would give me a basis from which to seek out the best form of treatments available to help my son.

Of course, I also needed to determine what else was wrong, and, again, I had a gut feeling that there was something else in addition to the ADHD, but did not know what. My earlier research had indicated that ADHD, in many cases, can co-exist with other conditions. We had observed, for example, that Daniel appeared to be much farther behind in most tasks, when compared to other children of a similar age. Although it was difficult for the medical practitioners to advise a further diagnosis at the age he was then, two years later, when Daniel was four years old, he was finally additionally diagnosed as having learning difficulties, a speech defect, and challenging behaviours. My wife and I had been aware that the challenging behaviours existed, but felt there was somehow more to it than this. This further diagnosis of learning disability and challenging behaviours was therefore another step in the right direction.

As an aside, by 'challenging behaviours', I mean truly challenging behaviours; such behaviours that were completely unacceptable yet equally unstoppable, day after day and night after night, with virtually no let up. Daniel slept very little and, at the very most, he could only manage a couple of hours of sleep – and that was on a good night. It was utterly heartbreaking to witness our son unable to burn off all his inner energy. If anyone had tried to explain to me, before I had personally witnessed this and experienced it, the devastation of the ADHD condition, I would never have understood in a million years of how terrible it really is, or indeed the huge impact that it has on all the members of a family. Bafflingly, there is still a minority of people who are actually of the opinion that the condition does not exist, believing instead that the children affected by the disorder are just naughty children. This is, of course, actually a million miles from the truth, and the condition most certainly does exist. Back as far as 1845, a German poet and physician named Heinrich Hoffman wrote books that described children with inappropriate behaviours and their compatibility with ADHD, and in particular one book about 'fidgety Philip', which was the story of a very hyperactive young boy, and, although children way back then were known to be hyperactive, it was not specifically diagnosed as ADHD until many years later.

Returning to Daniel's story, it was when he was around four years old that the destructive side of his condition really started to 'kick in'. Our family home became the setting for his terrible temper tantrums, such much so that most items in the house were destroyed at one time or another, and every day would see excrement smeared on the walls of both the bedrooms and the living areas. Tears would fall from my wife's eyes as the situation deteriorated from day to day, and friends and family slowly edged away from visiting our family home, many of them concerned that their vehicles would be targeted for destruction as ours was on many occasions. Car windows were smashed, number plates ripped off, huge scratches stood out in the paintwork. At times I felt as if, on the spur of the moment, I could have snapped and killed him, but then, just as quickly, I would recall that these behaviour problems were beyond Daniel's control – and we knew that we were unable to stop him, irrespective.

We attempted punishing him on many, many occasions, but nothing worked. It's not as simple as saying 'smack his backside'; a child who does not suffer from challenging behaviours and ADHD probably can be taught by very firm discipline, but children with some neurological disturbances who suffer from such behaviours are, indeed, very difficult to correct, hence the label of 'challenging' behaviours. Daniel quickly became labelled as an 'out of control' child, a child with whom, many told us, we would never be able to do anything. But the more that people told us this, the more determined I became to prove them all wrong, even if it meant a lifetime's devotion. After all, our son did not ask to be born with all these difficulties, and he deserved to be given all the opportunities that life had to offer. I often find it particularly sad that ADHD is entirely unlike, say, a physical deformity in a child in that it cannot be seen; a physical disability often can, and while children with a discernable physical condition are generally treated sympathetically, ADHD children are very often offered little sympathy and, in fact, many are disliked, in some cases to the extreme. My experience of children with the disorder is that they are generally extremely affectionate kids who just need to be understood and loved too. Furthermore, ADHD children can often be singularly gifted individuals, with many sufferers being remarkably intelligent.

That said, it can be difficult to keep this in mind, even as a parent, when confronted with an ADHD child's challenging behaviours. Each day and each night became a constant struggle as we fought to control Daniel, who was becoming uncontrollable – and all because of the most horrific of birth traumas. Almost every night, the his terrible reign of destruction in our home continued, and, amidst the sorrow and frustration that were by now seriously affecting my wife and I, it would have been a godsend to have been able to just pick up the phone and ask for help: someone to come over and take Daniel out, just for a couple of hours, but there was no-one, no support. Just a single hour would have made a huge difference, and would certainly have helped Daniel to calm down as well as giving us that short break in which to re-charge our batteries, ready for the next tantrum.

Then, just as we thought that things could not get any worse and after we had endured weeks of non-stop torment, stress and sorrow, someone would knock on our door and complain about something that Daniel had done. Sometimes, the complaints were relayed in a polite way, but, at other times, they were presented in a way that really was inappropriate, and which of course only added to our problems and was something we just did not need. However, I can now say that having a gifted son like Daniel has made me so much more a person who understands the problems facing others in similar circumstances. Before, I would have had no idea how families struggle to cope with an ADHD youngster who suffers from learning difficulties and challenging behaviours, and I could never have imagined that life could be so very different from a 'normal' way of family life. Every day with our son was entirely taken up with his particular needs, much more so than was the case with our other children, and every night became a battle for peace and quiet, a battle that we constantly lost. Harmony and calm in our family had become a thing of the past, as people passing by our family home were increasingly aware. Daniel could often be heard letting off steam, which took some people by surprise, but what had initially caused embarrassment soon became a standard way of life for us. Trust me, if we were unable to put up with being embarrassed, then the battle to help Daniel reach his full potential would probably have been lost before it had even fully begun; it simply wasn't an option.

All the tasks that Daniel attempted appeared to be so very distant from the 'norm'; for example, while other children would sit still, he would not, and when other children would make eye contact with their parents, he would not, and where other children played nicely with one another, Daniel would not. In fact, he found it extremely difficult to relate to their ways; while playing contentedly with toys was, for him, also a no-go area as he much preferred to destroy the playthings, and, perhaps most significantly, he appeared to be utterly distant from those who loved him so much, and especially my wife and I. As Daniel got older still, the battle became much tougher, with the family home still bearing the brunt of the aggressive side of his nature. Doors were not smashed through but ripped from their hinges; televisions were picked up as if they were feathers and thrown down, smashing into many pieces; settees were ripped to bits: nothing, absolutely nothing, was exempt from destruction. It became hell on earth, a hell that was constant and without pity. The one positive aspect of the damage to our home, which was owned by the local council, was that the housing inspector understood the difficulties we were having and the breakages were always repaired free of charge. If we had been required to pay for this ourselves, then we would probably have still been paying out to this day. Of course, it was something over which we had no control and, again, punishing Daniel had no effect, simply because it was all far beyond his power, too, although there were inevitably a few occasions when we did attempt to reprimand him, simply out of frustration and anger.

One of the organisations involved with our family suggested that, whenever Daniel's temper tantrums were really bad, we hold him down to the ground forcefully until he calmed down. This proved a futile effort, however, and did absolutely no good. In fact, by the time we gently released our hold of him, his anger would have become, actually, far worse, and a breakage of some sort would almost certainly follow. It is difficult to determine the best way forward with managing these behaviours, as much as they can be managed, as each child with ADHD is an individual and so where a form of restraint might work with one child, it could make another child worse. It should also be borne in mind that, whatever form of punishment is attempted, it is extremely difficult to stop entirely the challenging behaviours that are often associated with the ADHD

By this time, for us, it had reached a stage where Daniel's behaviour was not only challenging and destructive but also a real danger; to himself and to others. One of the more dangerous things that he had taken to doing was to try and find out what it would be like to get run over. Day or night, and whenever we turned our backs on him for a second, he would go out and lie in the middle of the road. Fortunately, we always managed to reach him before he found the painful or even fatal answer to his question, but one of these instances was nonetheless very, very close indeed. Although not actually laying in the road, he had run out of our drive and straight into the path of an oncoming car. It was a dark, foggy evening and I was unable to catch him before he reached the road. The car skidded and swerved sharply to avoid hitting Daniel; how the driver managed to miss him was a miracle. My heart was in my mouth; I really thought that he was going to make contact with the vehicle. When I later asked Daniel why he had done this, he replied, 'I want to die'. Boy, did this bring tears to my eyes, even though it was fairly likely that, at the age he was then, he did not really understand the concept of death, nor how serious and permanent it was.

3 Treatments: medication

We dreaded the thought of our young son taking medication, especially the 'mind-altering' drugs that actually can change the way you think, but also knew that something desperately needed to be done – and done sooner rather than later, or Daniel would surely finish up being very seriously injured or even killed. A huge number of people need to take drugs for various medical disorders, such as diabetes, and the medication available to assist with mental health issues are really no different. I have heard comments like, 'I would not allow my child to take these types of drugs', but at the end of the day it is really not that simple a decision; would you deny insulin to your child if they suffered from diabetes and you were recommended the drug by a doctor? Of course not. In fact, I, too, was initially absolutely against giving our son 'stimulant'-type medication, but there are many factors that need to be weighed up against one another when making such a decision.

After further research into the ADHD condition, I became aware that many youngsters who suffer from the disorder actually do much better on medication than their counterparts; nevertheless, the decision regarding our son taking medication was not taken lightly. Day after day, we would witness Daniel hurting himself after some silly accident; by way of example, another one of his favourite tricks at that time was to sprint down the garden path and then not stop in time to prevent himself from making contact with the wall. The ensuing injuries commonly required medical attention as, for some reason, Daniel never put his arms up to prevent his face making contact with whatever he ran into, which meant that he received some fairly severe wounds. Daniel's reflexes were so much slower than they should have been, as these particular reactions confirmed. His co-ordination was very bad, too, which only added to the injuries that he would sustain. Hospital visits were therefore commonplace, and, after having some of the more serious injuries attended to, we would always feel as though we were suspected of abusing him, simply because of the number of times we attended the Accident and Emergency department. Thankfully, the paediatrician, amongst others, knew how particularly prone Daniel was to self harm, not least as he had witnessed our son hurt himself in his consulting room on more than one occasion.

Daniel was eventually started on two types of medication: a stimulant-type drug commonly known as methylphenidate (specifically, the formulation branded as 'Ritalin', which had quite a bit controversy associated with it at the time) and an antipsychotic medication. While there were benefits, there were also downsides, especially with the antipsychotic medications, side effect for which included terrific weight gain and incontinence to name but a couple. In fact, these were so bad that we could not allow our son to continue taking the antipsychotics. However, Ritalin seemed tolerable, for the most part, and actually helped him to a certain degree, especially in the classroom situation, where it seemed to give him a short 'window of opportunity' in which to learn, and a 'short' window was better certainly better than none at all. Ritalin did also have its side effects, though, such as the fact that it made sleep difficult, and also seemed to have a 'rebound' effect, in which the hyperactive behaviours and the temper tantrums were worse on occasions. However, on balance, we considered that the benefits did outweigh the side effects, and that Ritalin was worth continuing with.

Daniel was also prescribed a drug called 'Bio-Melatonin'; Melatonin is a hormone and antioxidant that is produced naturally by the brain and other tissues. It is issued by the body when darkness falls, and, within an hour or two, the maximum amount will have been delivered. In Daniel's case, the Bio-Melatonin helped by reducing the time it took for him to get to sleep – not least as the Ritalin had been keeping him awake.

4 'Can't you control your child?'

A social worker visited our home on a regular basis at this time and, during one of her appointments, we explained how concerned we were becoming about Daniel continuously escaping the confines of our back garden whenever he had the opportunity. I was finding it increasingly difficult to catch him on such occasions, as he ran like the wind while I, being a smoker at the time, was very quickly gasping for breath. Meanwhile, our financial situation at the time was dreadful, to say the least, and so to have a fence erected around the back garden was, for us, way beyond our means, as the council house in which we lived had a large rear garden, and so would have required an extensive amount of material to encircle it securely.

The social worker contacted the council directly with regards to them erecting a fence, reassuring us that the local social services team would meet the cost. Finally, after a few weeks had passed, a workman arrived at our home, tools in hand, and began erecting the fence; it was an 8-foot-high chain-link construction complete with 4"-by-4" posts concreted into the ground. When the fence was all completed, which took just over a week, our back yard resembled a prisoner-of-war camp (indeed, we referred to it as 'Colditz'), but, nevertheless, as we looked out upon it with joy: here was our 8-foot-high fence, complete with a gate that we were able to lock, and we felt as though we could relax a little more and that the fence would surely contain Daniel and keep him safe. Such thoughts as these of containment and relaxation were soon to be proven to be premature, though, as we certainly had completely underestimated the climbing skills of Daniel. I watched him go running past our kitchen window, having scaling the chain-link wired fence, and escape to the great outdoors; from there, the options for him were endless, with distance proving to be no barrier either.

If an 8-foot-high fence could not contain him, then what would? What was the answer? It was then that another one of my bright ideas sprang to mind: 'Why not add 2 feet of extra chain-link wire onto the top of the fence, making it 10 feet high?' Surely, this would contain him? And so, after scrimping and scraping and missing out on a few, less important things, we collected enough money for the cost of the extension. A journey down to the local hardware shop was completed with the purchase of two rolls of 2-foot-high chain-link fencing, and then it was back home for the erection of the extension. As I was adding it, Daniel was scaling the fence, so it was a case of doing a bit of fencing, and then doing a bit of chasing. Once the task was completed, however, I made comments to my wife along the lines of 'if he scales that fence now, then I will eat my hat'. Guess what? 'Hats don't taste nice.' We could only but watch and wait – and it wasn't too many hours before he was up and over the newly extended fence. We then knew that the higher we went with the fence, the higher Daniel would climb to 'escape', which of course only added to the danger, and so we reverted to keeping watch on him constantly and never allowing him to go out into the back garden on his own.

Window locks were also needed, and all windows, for the most part, kept shut; otherwise, without doubt, Daniel would have leapt out of any of them, even from the first floor (which, with a drop of over 20 feet to the ground, could have had devastating consequences), mainly because he could not truly see any danger in anything. This was the case for many years, and even the 'stranger–danger' scenario meant nothing to him; for example, if he was given the opportunity, he would try to get into peoples' cars if they had stopped at traffic lights. Several times, we had to struggle with him to prevent him from entering the cars, and not only was this potentially dangerous, it was also at times embarrassing, especially as some drivers would give us a mouthful and pass comments such as, 'Can't you control your child?'. To be truthful, we could not control him, and neither could anyone else; our son was fast developing into a very *un*controllable child.

Social services were increasingly showing quite a keen interest in Daniel, which made my wife and I feel very uncomfortable as it appeared to us as if the team were somehow waiting for the right time to remove him from the family home. They were certainly well aware of the very real threat of him hurting himself, as well as of him possibly hurting others. There were several occasions where I felt that I needed to tell lies about how difficult things really were at home, such were our concerns about Daniel being removed to a 'more containing environment' as once was suggested by a child psychiatrist. The prospect of our son being removed from our home permanently was unthinkable, and so we dared not tell anyone about the dangerous objects that were often thrown around the room, for example, including kitchen knives of all descriptions (we finished up only buying the round-headed type of knives to eat our food with, and any sharp or pointed knives we had at home we threw out). Nor did we ever mention the attacks on his siblings, which would usually occur during one of his temper tantrums. There were many other things that we dared not to mention, in fact, because of our fear of Daniel's removal from home. Also, I continued to feel confident within myself that these attacks could surely be overcome if we put in further time and effort to help him, even if it would take many years to achieve. But, no matter what, we were determined to do our utmost to support him through this very difficult time he was going through.

My opinion of social services was at an all time low at this point, though. Why could they not help families who were facing extreme stress and difficulty coping, as we obviously were, by offering support? Rather, that is, than apparently giving such families additional worries? Was it all in my mind about the social services gathering information in preparation for such a time that they could remove our son? Although I cannot ever really answer that question with 100 per cent certainty, there was an event that occurred in our home which resulted in them calling me into their offices to discuss it, and which gave me the suspicion that this was their intention. Had I been truthful during the course of our discussions then, I suspect the consequences would probably have been very serious, with a good chance that Daniel would be taken from us and placed into the care system; a resolution that would not have, I feel sure, been in his best interests. These kids need unconditional love and support and nobody can love a child as parents do; many children placed in care actually do far worse than if they had remained at home – although, clearly, in some cases, children do actually need to be placed in a 'safe environment' away from the family home.

ADHD is not an automatic candidate for respite support for the diagnosed individual's carers – despite the fact that such care is provided for cases or conditions featuring less severe manifestations and issues -- and this is, I believe, where the problem lies. In order to secure even a small amount of respite support, we did have we had to shout loud and with the support of other professionals who were involved in our family's ongoing problems; a nurse from the community mental health team for people with learning difficulties spoke out very strongly about respite on our behalf, for example, and on one particular occasion she really threw it at the social services' representative, saying that, 'This family had been let down by the services time and time again', and adding, 'They are offered nothing. It's totally unacceptable.' Her input actually started the ball rolling towards regular meetings regarding respite. Initially, it was always a case of 'meetings', but that's as far as it went, at least for a few months, and we were always told that it was down to funding, which it may well have been the case, but there was also a shortage of people within the caring profession. (From our experience, at least, if a child with challenging behaviours is allocated a carer, then they would almost certainly need to be very fit and healthy person, amongst other criteria!)

We tried on numerous occasions to enjoy a relaxing family holiday together, but things never went according to plan and we would always return home after just a couple of days away. Imagine, if you can, setting off on holiday and, the moment that you arrive at your destination, your child running straight into the sea, fully clothed, then coming out wet and rolling in the sand and, when you try to catch him, he runs away as fast as he can and gets lost, leaving the confines of the holiday complex, which he did both day and night, upsetting other holiday-makers with 'inappropriate behaviours'. Imagine overhearing people using foul language against your child, unaware of the difficulties he or she is suffering from. Imagine other people demanding that you 'control your child'. Imagine being too afraid to take your child into the shops, and into the entertainment complexes in the evenings; not only afraid of others' reactions, but worried sick about all the things he could, and would, get up to at these places. Unlike a 'normal' family's holiday, we were unable to, for example, go into a club and enjoy the music and have a relaxing drink; all we could do was to admire other people enjoying themselves and be envious. Little did many really understand how very lucky they were, we thought, and how unfamiliar they must be with families like ourselves. By this point, of course, we had been in embarrassing situations so many times that we had actually become a little bit hardened to it, but, nevertheless, we still felt humiliated.

Again, the 'problem' goes back to these disorders not presenting themselves as a physical disability would: it's the unseen 'devil within'. Imagine your child using foul language – a common issue for many ADHD individuals – especially in public, with people looking on and passing judgements, and not understanding how utterly futile and frustrating such a response is, given that neither the parents nor the child are able to control such outbursts. Imagine going into shops and your child knocking items off of the shelves, ripping open packets of foods and eating the contents, completely unaware that it is wrong to do so, even though you have explained it so many times previously, and then staff asking you to leave the premises, sometimes politely or, at other times, not so politely. Each time, I felt like crying, and every single day soon became a sad day, as depression fell down into the very depths of my mind. I hated the world and I often thought to myself, 'What's the point of it all?'. I wished, at times, that the world would end, but then I would think of our son trying to cope in life without either myself or my wife to support him. 'How will he get by in this harsh world on his own?' These were my re-occurring thoughts then, and I expect that that final concern will remain with me for the rest of my life.

5   Just another label?

It was when Daniel was almost 14 years of age that he was further diagnosed as suffering from an autistic spectrum disorder, following a detailed examination by a clinical psychologist. Autism is typically diagnosed much earlier in life, usually when the individual is four years old or so. Somehow Daniel had slipped through the net, but did it really make any difference? Was it just another label? Well, although we had by now been offered a small amount of respite care (corresponding to the management of his ADHD disorder and associated behaviours), the autism diagnosis put us into a much stronger position to request additional support. Had the autism been diagnosed when Daniel was much younger, I am sure that we would have been able to access a sufficient amount of respite in the first place – respite that was so urgently needed.

The support that we were eventually offered took place on a Saturday when Daniel visited with a 'link family'. At first, we felt apprehensive about his leaving, mainly because we were concerned that he might hurt himself. However, it was only for a day (I usually picked him up to return home at around eight o'clock in the evening) and didn't take place every week, and the breaks would give us time to 'recharge our batteries', so to speak. It was always sad watching him go, though; he never looked back or waved goodbye to acknowledge us. He lived in his own little world, a world that he found extremely difficult to understand.

In fact, we were really pleased to have some respite on those occasional Saturdays, especially after a particularly difficult week; it gave us time to complete all those tasks that are usually taken for granted, such as shopping, which we were then able to do without any problems. Had it not been for those little breaks, I feel sure that we would have gone completely off our heads. Sadly, though, they weren't to last as, after just a short time, the lady from the link family was hit in her car by a drunken driver and suffered very serious injuries. And, obviously, further to horrific damage and harm inflicted upon her, that drunk driver was also directly responsible for our family losing the only small break we had at that time. Needless to say, our opinion of the drunken driver was very low indeed.

After a couple of months, social services arranged for Daniel to be given the chance to attend a local activity centre during the summer holidays for one day a week. The group insisted on a one-to-one support worker going with Daniel as a condition of his attendance, which was duly arranged. However, after just a couple of visits, he was expelled following an incident in which he rocked a boat over that had four children on board whilst they were all having a pleasure trip. We were informed this expulsion was undertaken purely for the safety of the other children, which we obviously understood, but we also felt sorry that our son could no longer attend, as he would have enjoyed all the activities. But, it had to be – even after I asked the group if they would be willing to give him one more chance.

Over the years, I did notice that, although there are many schemes for children with learning difficulties and special needs, there are far less for children who have challenging behaviours. (Wonder why?!) However, with this respite of one day a week ending quite abruptly, a charitable organisation – the Mid-Suffolk Holiday Opportunity Play Scheme, known as 'HOPS' – offered Daniel a chance to attend their centre. As before, one of the conditions of attendance was that he had a one-to-one support worker with him at all times, which was once again arranged. This activity centre was run during the summer holidays, with Daniel being offered two days a week, and so I would drop him off at a small town in the mornings at 09.30 and pick him up at 15.30 on the following afternoon. This was great – two days of unwinding! Unbelievable! Things went a little better with this group for Daniel, too, although they soon reached a stage where they were really struggling for funding. They arranged various fund-raising events in a bid to secure more financial support, and these functions continued throughout the year; I, too, racked my brains thinking of ways to help to support the group and came up with the idea of having a good haircut, such as a head shave. So, at one of the HOPS events, I sat in a chair with a lady beside me, clippers in hand, as another lady held a large glass jar into which people put donations. I was surprised at how much money was raised just by having a good haircut, with people throwing in coin after coin. One older lady (she must have been more than 90 years old) came and spoke to me as she handed over a £20 note, which, a few years ago, was quite a sum; she informed me that the charity was very close to her heart as she, too, had a family member who had special needs, and I thought to myself, 'What a lovely gesture'. It reinforced my belief that there are a lot of very pleasant people in this world.

6 An 'uncontrollable child'

Visits to the hospital with Daniel were, by this point, becoming an absolute nightmare. When all the other young children would sit still with a hospital support worker at a table in the waiting area painting, reading books, or taking part in other similar activities, Daniel would be running wildly through the corridors and wards with myself in hot pursuit, sometimes assisted by nurses, too. Looking back, I can see a humorous side to it all, but, at the time, it was certainly not funny: it was hell, especially when a doctor's consulting room was almost totally destroyed, with the doctor's stethoscope being ripped off of his neck by Daniel and flung across the room, after which he began jumping up and down on the examination couch as if it were a trampoline, the door was kicked repeatedly, and the doctor's notes were scattered everywhere. It must have looked like something out of a comedy film. The doctor went on to say, in a subsequent report, that his consulting room was almost totally destroyed in a matter of minutes, adding that Daniel was an 'uncontrollable child' who would eventually need to be in a more controlling or containing environment; a judgment that reinforced the opinions of others who were involved at the time and exacerbated our family's concerns, too. As soon as these dreaded hospital visits were finally reduced to one every few months, Daniel was then required to visit a child psychiatrist at a specialised clinic – and these visits proved to be just as difficult. In fact, I always had no option but to put my chair in front of the door to prevent him from 'escaping', as, given the chance, he would certainly have fled towards the great outdoors.

This was also the time when I had no choice but to give up my employment. We had reached a point where it took both my wife and I to care for our son, such was his demanding nature; we needed to give him the full support that he required, now and in the future years, and we both knew that we had a long, hard journey ahead of us, along a road that was surely marked by heartache after heartache along the way. Almost every task Daniel attempted was difficult for him; even eating his food correctly proved problematic, mainly because when he fed himself he tended to overfill his mouth to the extent that the food would fall from his mouth constantly. This, in turn, presented its own hazards, and so either my wife or myself would have to feed Daniel for his own safety.

Everywhere that we took our son, we tried to keep him safe and under control using, for example, his 'reins' – a harness-type fabric that had buckles at the back – but, although these are designed to be a containing piece of equipment, Daniel soon learnt how to 'escape' merely by lifting his arms up to a vertical position and then sliding down. After a short time, therefore, the reins became redundant, and it was simply a case of holding him firmly as we could – but even this presented us with problems, especially if he wanted to break free for a particular reason, such as going into a shop or whatever.

Wherever we went, people would stop and stare in amazement, and sometimes disbelief, as they witnessed our son having one of his now daily temper tantrums; tantrums that we were unable to prevent or curtail however hard we tried. We had certainly exhausted all the advice that we were given by a number of agencies, but absolutely nothing worked. In any case, and it was all to do with messages and signals deep inside his brain, and, although it may be relatively easy to stop inappropriate behaviours in most children, with ADHD children, it's a whole new ball game, as any parent of an ADHD child will confirm. Rules cannot be adhered to for any specific amount of time and the child seems, in many cases, to be able to remember and process simply the here and now.

The one positive thing that Daniel really enjoyed messing about for any length of time was anything that concerned mechanics, and so we encouraged him to focus his attention on such things. It helped him tremendously, at times, to keep his mind occupied – and, for as long as he was occupied, he was an absolute little angel sent from the heavens, the 'perfect child' you might say. I would often catch myself thinking, 'This would be wonderful if he behaved like this most of the time', yet I knew it would probably never be the case. However, when I did participate in anything that concerned mechanics, Daniel would love to help, whether it was tinkering with the family car, or pulling my mower apart, or any other similar mechanical tasks. If I was laying beneath my car, doing some repair task, Daniel would quickly join me (although there were times that I did not need any 'help' and would have preferred to have gotten on with the task at hand!). We purchased a workshop manual for lawnmowers and started buying Daniel old mowers from the dump for a couple of quid a throw. That money was very well spent as, after just a few months, he quickly understood how to take the mowers apart. And although, at first, Dad had to put them back together again... he would always watch me do so and was soon able to put them back together again himself. Relatively quickly, he became skilled enough to repair mowers confidently, and this actually occupied his mind for some time. As he became older and a little more mature, a few people in the village would bring their mowers to him for any repairs that they needed doing. Daniel loved to hear the sound of the engines running after he had been able to get a mower repaired, having spent a few hours tinkering with it; in fact, this became a constant noise in my back garden, hour after hour, the revving up of engines, the fumes, but we knew that, therapeutically, it was a good and positive thing for him.

We ended up purchasing him a large shed-come-workshop so that he would be able to continue his hobby in comfort, rather than working outside in all weathers, as he would be outside with his mowers, come rain or shine. But then he began to start up mowers in the early hours of the morning, which was part of the impulsive side of his nature and one of the characteristics of ADHD. He would just wake up at times like 03.00 a.m., go downstairs and out to his shed; it did not matter to him if he was dressed or not – in fact, he usually went outside in his 'birthday suit'. He would then start up the mowers and rev them up to full capacity. Needless to say, up got Dad then outside to stop him, which, in turn, would soon kick off one of Daniel's temper tantrums, and then our peace would all be gone, especially when I tried to get him to come back indoors. People living in close vicinity to our home would come to their windows and look out to see what all the commotion was; some were understandably quite unhappy at being woken up at 03.00 in the morning. I knew they were in the right, and they certainly had a very good reason to be annoyed. In fact, I felt equally as annoyed at being woken up also, although at that time my wife and I were usually woken up night after night in any case, and in a peculiar sort of way this for us eventually became the norm. I could not imagine then what it would be like to have a decent night's sleep; it had all become a luxury of yesteryear.

Looking back at all of the various meetings we held at our home – with psychiatrists, mental health team members, psychologists, education workers to name a few – I cannot really say whether any made a difference to the eventual outcome for our son. Some of the advice we received was most helpful at times, and did assist us in some respects, although of course there was nothing that could be done by any organisation that would eradicate the behaviour problems, which was really the core issue.

We did have two people who lived close by to us and who really understood our situation, and they would always ask if they could be of assistance to us when times were really bad. They always knew when those times were occurring and Daniel was having one of his major temper tantrums as they could hear him quite easily as he shouted and screamed out at the top of his voice. One of these ladies also had a relation who suffered from behaviour problems and this obviously made her much more understanding with regard to our situation, and more willing to assist us. It was always good to know that there were some kind and considerate people out there who were willing to help our family at times such as these.

Of course, we took positive action ourselves, too, as a family. For example, as time passed, we realised that it was not really an ideal situation allowing Daniel to sleep in the same room as my wife and I and so, against our better judgements, we purchased some bunk beds so that Daniel could sleep in the same room as his older brother, Luke. However, this soon became clear that this was far from the solution that we were hoping for as arguments quickly erupted between Daniel and Luke. Hardly a night would pass without conflict between the two boys, but we understood what the cause of the problem was: whereas Luke was trying to get good night's sleep, Daniel was wide awake and playing computer games, watching television, and running about. Then came the shouting from Luke: 'Dad, come and get Daniel – he's keeping me awake!' After going into the boys' room and settling Daniel down, all became quiet again– but only for a short time, and no sooner had I got back into bed, then I would have to get up after it would all flare up again: 'Dad, come and get Daniel!' We eventually had no choice than let Daniel come back into our bedroom again as, rather than him disturb his brother, it was obviously a better arrangement to allow him to disturb my wife and I. And so, back to 'normal'. Why we decided even to give it a go, we will never know: it should have been obvious to us, in the first place, that he would disturb his brother? I imagine that we just hoped that things would had improved, which certainly they had and did not. Daniel back in our bedroom with us was still not an ideal scenario, though, and while we loved the house and village where we lived, we decided that the only real option we had was to move into a more practical home – with an extra bedroom.

The thought of moving was a little daunting, simply because most of the people in the village where we lived understood that we had a young son with behavioural problems and most of them had come to know our son and had a certain degree of patience with him. One of our very real concerns was that, if we moved out into new area and a new home, it would be like starting from scratch again. Our choices, however, seemed limited. A representative from the social services team suggested to the council the possibility of building an extension onto our home, rather than re-housing us, but the local council declined, adding that it would be cheaper to re-home us than to build an extension for use as an extra bedroom. We understood this as it made sense, but what if we moved and people were not as understanding as those in the area we were leaving? Would we have to move again? And again? Nevertheless, after waiting on the housing list for six months, we were duly offered another home with an extra bedroom, and so, reluctantly, we moved. It was a sad time for us in ways, and when the house was empty and I walked through each room one by one for the final time, my mind reflected back over all the previous years at the house. I remembered when we first moved in, and I remembered back to the time I bought Daniel home from the hospital after his stay. I looked at the doors, which had been subjected to the most severe of our young son's abuses, and many of which were therefore filled and painted over to hide up their battle scars. Looking at the high chain-link fence that we referred to as 'Colditz' made me wonder if the new occupants would comment on such a high fence? Our next-door neighbours came over with a bottle of wine and wished us luck in our move and the best for Daniel, and said that they hoped his problems will be less severe as he gets older – and this was another of those times that I found very touching.

We had not been settled in our new home for many weeks before the complaints began arriving. The first came after Daniel ran down the garden of one of the houses a few doors down and decided to try and discover what was inside the occupant's shed. Although I was searching for him at the time, I was actually looking in the wrong direction and, when I did eventually catch up with him, the neighbour was already understandably annoyed that our son had been in his yard, especially in his shed. It transpired that Daniel had actually tried to start the person's mower up. I was not given time to explain to the chap about our son's problems due to the hostile attitude I was greeted with; however, a few days later, another person explained to the gentleman that Daniel had learning difficulties and so on, and the chap who complained apparently regretted his actions and wished that he had said nothing.

Daniel was very keen on motorcycles and go-karts and, with this in mind, we purchased him an old moped and asked a local farmer if he had a field that was unused and on which he would allow my son to go 'scrambling'. He kindly allowed him to ride his moped on one of the nearby fields when the cutting of corn had finished, and I thought that this was brilliant, but, as I watched Daniel going round the field, he suddenly sped past me and onto the road. The hunt was on once again, but, this time, I had a problem insofar as the moped had more speed than my short legs, and so I watched in dismay as Daniel disappeared towards the horizon. After hours of searching, and then walking home to weigh up all the options, I decided the only real choice I had was to telephone the police. This was not a course of action that I liked, but Daniel's safety was paramount. As I picked up the phone, though, a knock came at our front door; on answering it, I was confronted by two men who seemed very angry. 'Has your son been riding a moped?' one of the men enquired. When I explained to them about him escaping to the highways, they informed me that he had upset their pheasants in their compound, adding that they would call the police if I did not find him. I explained that I was in the process of calling the police when they knocked on my door, but that I would continue the task when they had finished their conversation with me, and they eventually calmed down to some degree. Furthermore, one final look for our son prior to calling the police yielded results: he had run out of fuel and so, thankfully, the police were not involved. I dread to think what would have happened had there been an accident, what with no tax, no MOT, no insurance, underage driving... It is difficult to say how the police would have reacted, though, given the circumstances. Needless to say, Daniel would have no more mopeds! The next thing to hold his attention was go-carts, but similar problems occurred, even though he had promised to stay in the rear garden, and he really meant to keep his promise at the time, but the impulsive side of his nature would always spoil everything for him.

Daniel had also begun, for some reason, to make '999' emergency calls just for the sheer hell of it and, before long, police cars and fire engines started to appear outside of our home. We did manage to stop this particular behaviour by going off the main phone and resorting to the mobiles – not ideal, but the alternative may have had more serious implications. Also, a fire officer had spoken with Daniel about the seriousness of dialling '999' for non emergencies, and even took the precaution of fitting our home with a smoke alarm!

Other complaints had started coming our way, too; some concerning the noise that Daniel was making during his temper tantrums, and others about him knocking on people's doors and asking them if they had any old lawn mowers they did not want. His obsession with the lawnmowers had just grown and grown, but we really tried hard to explain to him that it is inappropriate to knock on neighbours' doors and ask for anything, let alone lawnmowers.

As the months went by, though, almost everyone in the village became familiar with Daniel and slowly began to accept him for who he was – everyone, that is, apart from a local bully who thrived on 'being tough'. Many came to like him, even giving him odd jobs such as grass cutting, hedge cutting, cleaning cars, or other tasks that they needed doing; one particular couple for whom Daniel started doing odd jobs for in the village still employ him part time today. Another elderly lady who lived close by also gave him regular part time work, but, sadly, has since died.

And so, with descriptions of his traumatic birth and his earlier years (about which only a few examples have, thus far, been written) here concluded, we move onto another event in our son's life. At first, we were undecided about it, but, in hindsight, we feel that we did the correct thing for him as we pursued a claim for 'medical negligence'.

7 A 'medical accident'

Although we had, and still have, the greatest respect for the medical profession, we also knew that we must not allow that respect to dissuade us from doing what we considered to be the right thing to do for our son – and, equally, the wrong thing – and there remained some issues that concerned us insofar as these had never really been explained to us in a way that my wife and I could make any sense of. For example, while we are not medically educated, we had nonetheless learned that if meconium (an infant's earliest stools) is observed during the labour period, it can be an indicator of foetal distress, often at a level that requires emergency medical intervention. Meconium was seen on a midwife's glove during an internal examination of my wife and while we did not know the significance of this at the time, we did later on.

My wife's pregnancy period was trouble free. Everything went smoothly right up until the birth of our son, so why he was eventually delivered suffering from such very serious problems, problems that were going to affect him, in all probability, for the entirety of his life? Another fact that made us a little uneasy was that, prior to my wife being admitted to hospital for the delivery, a doctor had explained that owing to my wife's ongoing health problems our baby would need to be delivered via a Caesarean section operation. A natural birth would, we were advised, be hazardous for her and for the baby. However, when my wife arrived at the hospital, two days later, at 07.30 a.m. in preparation for the planned operation, a different doctor had other ideas and suggested she opt for a normal delivery.

Our eldest son had been delivered by a Caesarean section and subsequently our daughter, too, and no problems occurred with either of those deliveries – everything had been fine – so, if our second son had also been delivered by a Caesarean section, might the outcome have been more positive than it actually was? We will never really know the answer to that question with any amount of surety. At the time, we felt that we had two choices: either we did nothing and just put it down to one of those unfortunate incidents that do occur from time to time, or, alternatively, we seek legal advice to try and establish the true and complete facts behind it all. It was a decision that we gave an enormous amount of thought to; if we did nothing, then would it be in the best interests of our son, who was unable to act for himself, and would we be able to live with the thought that all Daniel's difficulties were, possibly, down to an error in the birth delivery method and that we as parents did nothing about that? We also knew that securing legal advice on the issue would not repair the damage done to our son's brain; no matter what, it would not repair the learning disabilities, it would not heal the ADHD, it would not make the challenging behaviours less challenging, and it would not alleviate his autism. It could put our minds at rest, though, with the knowledge that we took what we considered to be the best course of action for our son.

We received lots of advice from friends and family members, none of which would, we decided, sway us one way or another as, however well intended, these people were not, and had not been in, our position. I firmly believe that you really have to be in such a position yourself in order to fully understand all the pros and cons. It's easy for individuals to pass comments such as 'seek legal advice', but it also should be borne in mind that such a course of action can, in many ways, make you feel guilty; it might make you feel ashamed of questioning people for whom you generally have such a huge respect. The road can be long and hard in such cases as, when you take action such as that that we were considering, it usually entails many years of visiting various medical experts and travelling, in some cases, to venues spread across the country, and you must be fully prepared for this at the onset. To go against a professional body, too, such as those involved in medicine, is really a very difficult step to take. Or, at least, these were the considerations in our particular circumstances and so to reach a decision about what to do for the best was really quite difficult. And so it was that, with Daniel's best interests at heart, we decided to consult with lawyers. Fortunately for us, young children are entitled to legal aid in their own right, with parents representing them; had this not been the case, then it would have been a non-starter in any event, as these cases can cost huge amounts of money, the sort of funds that were simply not available to us.

The first task that I really did not relish, once we'd made our decision, was to visit our family GP to inform him of our intentions. Initially, I experienced the anticipated feelings of guilt and, to some degree, regret – it made me feel like a nasty person – but these feelings were overtaken by feelings of sorrow for my son, which then made my task that little bit easier. The medical profession is, in my experience, a profession that sticks together – and this view was confirmed to me after reading a letter that our GP at the time sent to the local hospital advising the staff there of our intentions. We understood why this had been done, though, and indeed that the medical profession is not alone in being loyal to its associated members.

To achieve the most favourable results for our case, we obviously needed lawyers who were experienced in medical negligence, and so, with this in mind, I researched various contacts that might be able to offer us some information as to the best way forward. After all, it's not every day that you seek action for possible medical mishaps, and my wife and I were on completely new ground: we had never previously even considered any form of legal action for anything, let alone something as significant as this. I eventually was given the name of a London establishment known as 'AVMA' ('Action for the

Victims of Medical Accidents'; established in 1982, it has since changed its name, in 2003, to Action Against Medical Accidents), a charity that assists people who have suffered as a result of a medical accident. It recommends solicitors whose speciality is within the medical negligence fields, and normally will suggest a specialist team that is within easy travelling distance.

Although we live only 10 miles away from a large town that boasts many solicitors' practices, AVMA recommended a team of solicitors based 35 miles or so from our home address, purely because of their particular expertise in cases such as ours. On our first visit, we were introduced to the solicitor who would be in charge of our case, and his secretary and a nurse were also present. We were informed, by the solicitor, that the nurse was regularly in contact with many of the top UK hospitals and that she was highly skilled in issues concerning the birth of babies. Her visits to the hospitals in the capital were normally for the specific reason of looking into potential medical blunders. This nurse was no longer working for the health service, but was employed full time by the solicitor's practice.

This first visit went on for a very long time as a comprehensive explanation was needed surrounding the events of our son's birth, including details from the months leading up to the birth period. A secretary sat at her desk and wrote everything down that was said, word for word, throughout the consultation.

At the finish of this first meeting, the solicitor explained that he would need to retrieve all the medical records, both from the particular hospital concerned and also from our local GP's practice. He said that it would take approximately four to six weeks for these records to be sent over and for them to carefully study the files ahead of our next meeting. On many of the visits to the solicitor, I would ask myself again if we were taking the correct course of action and, again, feelings of guilt would often enter the equation. Indeed, during once such bout of guilt, we really felt like discontinuing with the case – just throwing in the towel and getting on with our lives, no more unwanted hassle – but then our thoughts turned back to our son, which, in turn, spurred us on with a new determination to continue with what we started until the end. Why should I have these feelings of guilt when I am only attempting to do what I feel is in my son's best interests? Surely, many parents would take the same course of action as my wife and I chosen? After all, we are, as parents, our child's protectors, aren't we?

During these early stages, my wife's health was increasingly becoming a concern, too, with diabetes being foremost amongst her medical problems at the time. In fact, her health had deteriorated to the extent that she was no longer able to accompany me on subsequent visits to the solicitor's office, or to any of the other venues that we were required to attend concerning the case, mainly because she found the travelling increasingly difficult and tiring. Daniel also did not need to attend many of the venues, which, given his inability to remain still, was probably a positive thing, as any serious discussions would have been very difficult to maintain if I was also constantly chasing after him.

A letter from the solicitor eventually came through our door with a date given for another meeting. This new appointment date was only a week later than the date on the letter, and so the ball had well and truly started rolling and things had now started to move at a reasonable pace. On the day of the visit, and after speaking with the solicitor, I was surprised to discover that some of the medical records concerning the events leading up to our son's birth had gone 'missing'. 'How could such relevant details go missing,' I thought to myself, but there was little I could do to discover why. It did make me feel even more suspicious to a certain degree, but, after much discussion regarding this, it was agreed that the truth as to what happened to the missing records would in all probability never be established. Of course, just how relevant these missing records would be to the eventual outcome, too, would never be known. I did find it 'unacceptable', but what could I do? It was simply a case of, 'Oh well, carry on regardless'. Nevertheless, because of this and other certain discrepancies, the solicitor felt that the case 'should proceed further'.

'We would like you to take Daniel to Middlesex Hospital in London for a detailed MRI scan on his brain to be taken and evaluated,' he explained.

'Why can he not go to the local hospital for the scan?' I asked.

'It's not really advisable to allow him to have the MRI scan at the same hospital as we are in conflict with,' replied the solicitor, which seemed to me to make sense. 'Furthermore, taking into consideration the difficulty he has in remaining still, we will require him to be sedated for the procedure. Are you agreeable to this?' he asked.

'Well, I think there is no alternative really, is there, and if it is going to be of further assistance, then yes, it must be done,' I replied. I did my best to explain to Daniel what was going to happen – he would be given a small injection in his hand that would not hurt him but that would make him sleep for a very short time – and he appeared to be OK with it all, although he probably did not fully understand.

A few weeks passed by and we soon found ourselves en route to the hospital. Once we arrived in the capital, I had to ask the way to the particular hospital to which we were going on a few occasions as my knowledge of London was indeed very limited, and there is actually more than one 'Middlesex hospital', I believe. I am not sure whether satellite navigation equipment was around in that day, although, even if it was, I certainly had not got the funds to afford such a luxury. I had only been to the capital, many years earlier, a few times to visit my younger brother who was being treated at the Great Ormond Street Hospital for Children, but, on this occasion, I was driving my car, whereas on my previous visits, I had gone by train and taxi, as I had not got a driving licence at that time. On reaching our destination, I was shocked to learn that to park my car for a few hours in the borough council car park would cost £22, which was quite a sum way back then; parking at the meters was a no go, due to the time limits and also not knowing for sure just how long we were going to be in the hospital.

When we eventually arrived at the hospital, things once again began to move quite fast. All the usual pre-operative tests were performed and, before I knew it, our son was under the anaesthetic and being wheeled into the room that housed the MRI scanner. It was not the period during which Daniel was fast asleep and under the anaesthetic that upset me, but, rather, the period when he drifted from a state of being wide awake to the unconscious state; that short period when the drug was introduced into his body and his eyes began closing, almost as if his life was over. It was a strangely touching moment that made tears well into my eyes which I was unable to control, no matter what.

The MRI scanner took detailed pictures of Daniel's brain, mainly by cross-sections. These images were then retrieved as 'pictures' similar to X-rays and would be forwarded to our solicitor, once they had been studied carefully and a conclusion reached. All in all, I found the day at the hospital quite overwhelming – especially when my mind was filled with thoughts concerning my son's future. Even then, I was trying to imagine how my son's life was going to be, in comparison to my own life. Would he have girlfriends? Would he ever get married? Would he ever be able to live independently? Would his behaviour problems allow him to steer clear of the criminal justice system? These were only a very few of the negative thoughts that not only entered my head at the hospital, but on almost a daily basis, and concerned me immensely.

A few weeks passed and it was back to the solicitor's office again. He gave us the news that the MRI scans had detected areas of abnormality deep within the brain, and, although this could not determine with 100 per cent accuracy if negligence had been a factor, it did determine that a degree of brain damage was obvious. So, this had been a positive step – although it was already obvious to my wife and I that Daniel was not on a par with his peers and that he experienced significant difficulties in his everyday life. However, the scan seemed to formally confirm that his brain had suffered from an insult and so, with this proven, the solicitor then suggested that I take Daniel to Sheffield to allow a thorough evaluation to be undertaken by a leading consultant neurologist. The outcome of this evaluation would determine once and for all if it was worth continuing with our quest. It was to be another step that would be the deciding factor regarding whether it all would end after the report from the neurologist was returned and studied, or, indeed, if it would continue to the next stage.

A neurologist is a highly trained medical professional who is experienced in diseases of the nervous system, including the brain, spinal cord, and all the peripheral nerves. The specialist that Daniel was to visit had also written books on ADHD, among other relevant topics. However, given all the neurologists who were situated much closer to our location than this one at Sheffield, I did wonder, 'Why travel all the way to consult with one at Sheffield?', which was quite a few hours' drive from our home. When I asked the solicitor this question, he explained to me that they normally worked alongside this gentleman, and that his experience in disorders such as those that Daniel was affected by was outstanding – and that he had, in addition, helped on many occasions to secure positive outcomes. The solicitor also felt confident that the neurologist would be completely independent from the health authority against which our concerns were levied.

We decided to hire a car for the journey, simply because we felt that our 15-year-old family car had a great possibility of breaking down en route, and we certainly wanted to avoid that scenario. This travelling around the country business was all new to me, and I much preferred the quiet, slow pace of country life, but, then again, it was all good experience for Daniel, especially if you disregarded the reason behind it all, and this time he obviously needed to attend. Once we arrived at the venue in Sheffield, the neurologist, a gentleman in his fifties of slim stature, asked Dan to perform lots of different tasks, some of which I could see were very difficult for him, when compared to other children of a similar age. It made me feel very sad when I witnessed him unable to balance as he should have done; it made me feel sad when I watched his co-ordination tasks; and it made me feel sad that, throughout the consultation, Daniel did not acknowledge me in any way. As ever, his own little world was all he was aware of, a world that would never be similar to my world, itself a place where autism, ADHD, and learning difficulties were not really given the consideration that they so deserved. Not only was Daniel given physical tasks to perform, but mental tests were also gathered. The neurologist filled page after page with information before explaining that his findings would be sent on in due course to our solicitor. He did, however, explain to me then that some of his findings would be of benefit if and when the case proceeded to the next step, and now it was all going to be in the hands of the solicitors. Would this be the finish or would it now go on to a meeting in the barristers' chambers at Crown Office Row in London.

It was not long before we knew the answer, and I was soon sitting in the offices of our solicitor as he explained to me that the report from the neurologist was 'positive' in most respects, and that the case was now going to the final step prior to the law courts, a consultation with the barrister, and the meeting was to be arranged with a host of other individuals, which would include barristers, solicitors, medical experts, and many reports from a variety of specialists that Daniel had visited in the years leading up to the meeting at the barristers' chambers. This would be where it all rested, from here it would either go to the law courts with a claim for medical negligence, or it would all end at the proposed meeting venue.

Daniel was not required to attend this particular meeting, which was understandable considering the delicate nature of the discussions; also, he would have found it impossible to remain still for the amount of time that the meeting would go on for. This time I decided that the train would be the best way to travel; just a train journey to London, then the relatively short taxi ride from the station to Crown Office Row.

Arriving at Crown Office Row, everything suddenly all seemed surreal: I observed a large archway and, beyond the archway, lots of offices, all of which were used by members of the legal profession, mostly barristers, and for me, a mere humble layperson, to arrive at such a place about which I previously had no knowledge and to go into a meeting with people of immense intelligence was beyond my imagination. It was an experience of a lifetime for me, and initially quite daunting.

I was greeted by a secretary who led me through to the conference room where another surprise met my eyes: a huge oval table with about 12 people seated around it, both male and female. First, a barrister introduced himself and shook my hand in an authoritative but friendly manner: 'Mr Collins, I am Mr [X] and I am your representing barrister.' He then introduced me to the rest of the people in the room, who included medics, neurologists, and specialist nurses, to name but some. In the corner of the room, an illuminated picture of Daniel's brain was to be the focusing point to begin with. Soon, things were being discussed that I had a problem relating to, although my barrister did his best in explaining things to me in detail as we went along. Indisputable evidence of Daniel's brain damage was a factor upon which all the professionals agreed, but this in itself was apparently not evidence of any medical negligence. However, it was discussed that negligence had certainly played a part in the actual birth trauma – but, still, there were concerns with regards to proving that negligence had played a part, that the outcome would have been any different had my wife had an emergency section to deliver our son, and this was where the major problem arose. It was to become the final stumbling block. Had additional medical problems surfaced in Daniel, such as cerebral palsy, then it would have been much more clear cut, and in all probability a positive outcome would have resulted. Mercifully, though, Daniel was not affected by this terrible condition, although many children who are starved of oxygen at birth do actually finish up with cerebral palsy. The talks went on and on, and there were disagreements concerning the issues of whether or not the case should go to trial; some were positive and others were not so.

The talks went on for almost four hours and the experts were undecided, initially, as to the next step. Finally, though, a conclusion was reached, as the barrister explained: 'Mr Collins, we feel that if the case should proceed to the law courts that it would be very difficult to prove specifically that, had other delivery methods been attempted, the outcome would have been any different. I suggest that this is as far as it should go. I appreciate that it must be difficult to accept being told that medical negligence had been in part responsible and yet nothing can be done about it, but, if we did go to the courtroom, the possibility of a successful outcome would indeed be very lucky, and would need to be proven on the "balance of probabilities", which is going to be extremely difficult.' He then asked, 'What is your opinion?', to which I replied: 'I have every faith in you and if that is your opinion then I will certainly go with that.'

'You have most certainly taken the correct course of action,' he advised, 'and can rest assured that you have acted in the best interests of your son'.

Although I felt disappointed and sad for Daniel, these words from the barrister lifted me up and confirmed that it was not really all about winning the case, but doing the best for my son, which I was confident that I had achieved. And so, after around five years of travelling the breadth and width of the country in pursuit of answers as to why our son was born as he was, all ended here on this cold autumn day; a negative result, but a worthwhile cause, and we could now rest assured that we did our best for Daniel.

On my way back home from this final meeting, I reflected on all the events surrounding the medical negligence claim. I recalled how difficult the decision was to pursue the case in the first place, and I remembered again all the different venues I attended with Daniel in connection with medical claim – the visit to Sheffield, the visit to the Middlesex Hospital, the countless visits to the solicitor's office, and, finally, the consultation in the barristers chambers – and although it felt a huge burden on occasions for Daniel and myself and wife, we all learned much from the experience. In fact, as I said previously it was an experience of a lifetime.

Daniel was a very young boy at the time, but he does remember most of the places we visited, although he cannot remember many of the individuals that were concerned in the case. He now fully understands what the claim was all about, and he appears to be completely satisfied with it all, including the outcome.

8   Treatments: Chinese medicine

We had previously very little knowledge of alternative medicines, and I personally only had faith in one form of healing and that was through the conventional medicines, but was this reason enough to deny our son access to other forms of treatment? What could be lost by it, apart from a few pounds? In fact, when you are desperately trying to help a loved member of your family, you are willing to try many things in the hope for a cure or, at least, improvements in their condition, and money considerations do not enter the equation, even if you have very little, which was the case with us.

The three particular alternatives of which we were aware were Chinese medicine, homeopathy, and faith healing. We decided that we would let Daniel, with his permission, have a trial period with each of them as, even if the end results were not positive, little could be lost by it, and we would never know if there were any benefits to be had unless it each was tried. We explained as best we could to Daniel about him going for these alternative treatments and the reasons behind it all, although we actually put it to him in such a way that he could perhaps understand more easily. We were always truthful to Daniel and we had already explained to him that he had suffered from a birth trauma and that some medical issues that affected him were as a result of this; although, again, we did not say to him 'you have suffered a degree of brain damage', but instead worded it as something along the lines of 'not enough oxygen reached your brain during your time of birth and this has unfortunately left you with some minor difficulties'. The difficulties at that time were, of course, far from minor.

It was never a case of discontinuing with the conventional medicine, but, instead, of using the alternatives in combination with it. It was also done in full agreement with the doctors whom Daniel was seeing at the time, including the child psychiatrist, who was particularly interested to find out if it was helping our son in any way, and so he was kept informed at each visit. The first alternative treatment that we decided to try was the Chinese medicine, but, first, I wanted to do some further research into this type of alternative medicine, just to make us all feel more relaxed about it, understand any safety issues, and to discover the best way to find a good practice.

During my research, I discovered that a widely used form of Chinese medicine is acupuncture, a technique that has been used for many, many years, and which involves inserting very fine needles into various locations on the body. It also involves the manipulation of the needles by turning them in a to-and-fro motion. The points of entry by the needles are known as meridians, and there are 12 main meridians, and 8 extra meridians.

Acupuncturists use disposable stainless steel needles that are generally sterilised with ethylene oxide gas, although, in some cases, other sterilisation methods are used. The needles used are also much smaller than the normal hypodermic needles as they are not hollow and do not need to inject fluids. The upper ends of the needles are thicker in circumference and are bound with a bronze wire or covered with plastic, which enables the acupuncturist to get a firm grip on the needle whilst also adding to each needle's strength. Most practitioners warm the needles when they are entered into the specific points on the body, and this is done by 'moxibustion', which is the burning of a variety of herbs, primarily mugwort, and, although this is actually a different treatment than acupuncture, it is usually used in combination.

I did note, during some of my research, that acupuncture has allegedly had great success in the treatment of musculoskeletal pain, such as arthritis, but that it should nonetheless be used as a complementary therapy. Yet, according to another particular study, acupuncture seems to alleviate pain just barely better than sticking needles into non-specific parts of the body, with the same study concluding that some of acupuncture's healing may be due to the 'placebo' effect.

As with any invasive procedure, there are risks with acupuncture, too, although these risks are low when receiving treatment from trained practitioners. The main risks are infections and so, by law, the needles used are

required to be sterile, disposable and used only once –
although, in some instances, the needles may apparently
be reused if they are re-sterilised.

However, I could find no studies that suggested
acupuncture to be of any benefit to individuals who had
suffered from brain damage; whether or not there is data
out there to support any such theory, I am unsure.
Nevertheless, we had started and so it was a case of no
turning back. We were initially going to allow our son
access to three alternative treatments and this was still
going to happen. And whilst I found no actual data to
support that it helped to repair brain damage, we were
unsure whether it might help Daniel in some other areas
of his life, such as his hyperactivity and his
impulsiveness, and would it show any benefits in helping
him sleep.

We made an appointment for Daniel to visit a
Chinese medical centre, after being recommended one in
a town a few miles from our home. The recommendation
was from a middle-aged lady who lived nearby and who
had been treated successfully at the centre for a smoking
addiction. On arriving at the centre, we were met by a
Chinese gentleman who was of slim stature and aged
between 50 and 55 years. He greeted us warmly before
writing down detailed notes of Daniel's birth and
subsequent problems. During this time, I was finding it
difficult in keeping Daniel seated, and from time to time
he managed to escape my grasp and flee. Nevertheless,

after a few 'escapes' I did manage to contain him, and so on we went with the consultation.

The practitioner inspected Daniel's face and was especially thorough on his examination of his tongue: he wrote down the tongue size, the shape of the tongue, coating, etc. He then asked for information regarding Daniel's taste, thirst, sleep, and defecation, amongst other things, and, all in all, his questioning was thorough and precise and he left very few stones unturned in his assessment.

Once all the questioning was completed, he suggested that if anything was going to help Daniel, then it would be the acupuncture, which is what we had initially thought, too. Chinese medicine is not just about acupuncture, and there are many other treatments on offer, but it is all tailored for individuals. The practitioner now asked Daniel to remove his shoes, socks, and top. As I held my son's hands, to help calm him, the practitioner undid some small sterile needle packs one by one, and then slowly introduced them to many specific points on Daniel's body, including his head, feet, arms, torso, and the webs and palms of his hands. When the needles reached the desired depth, I witnessed a slight twinge in the areas where the needles were introduced. The gentleman then began to turn the needles in sequence of a backward and forward motions and, at the same time, he applied a substance that heated the needles, which Daniel explained to me were pain free.

There were by now a number of needles protruding from Daniel's face and scalp, and yet not a single drop of blood had appeared. The procedure took around 35 to 45 minutes, and then, one by one, the needles were withdrawn and placed in a disposable bin. We were recommended some herbal-type tea, which cost £10 per pack, and told that it might help in calming Daniel down and, possibly, help him to sleep better.

The cost per visit, which was on a weekly basis, was £20, with an extra £10 per fortnight for the herbal tea. The child psychiatrist was keeping a close watch on Daniel in the meantime, but nothing appeared to be changing: he was still extremely hyperactive, he was still destructive, and he was still not sleeping for any decent amount of time. But we knew that we had to give this treatment cycle a fair crack of the whip and allow enough time for it to work.

Friends and family would pass comments such as 'what a waste of time' or 'waste of money' and some even referred to it as 'a load of mumbo jumbo'. Deep in my mind, I had similar thoughts, but I imagine I was still 'clutching at straws'. Other friends would pass positive comments, such as 'worth a try', as they understood how very desperate our situation was at the time.

Week followed week of attending the clinic, and week after week we noticed no improvements. The acupuncture did not appear to be having any effect on our son's condition whatsoever. Even after visiting the medical centre for two months, nothing had changed, and, after such a time span, if anything was going to change then, in reality, we surely could have expected to see some improvements within this time, however small, and so it seemed that the only real option we had was to stop the visits. At least we had given it a fair chance, and this stop then presented us with the second of the alternative treatment options to try for our son, namely homeopathic remedies.

9 Treatments: homeopathy

First of all, it was back to the research routine and trying to find out a little bit of background information regarding this alternative treatment's success rate, and indeed its safety. Through my research, I discovered that, for example, homeopathy is an alternative medicine that is supposed to work by treating the patients with extremely diluted preparations that are thought to cause effects similar to the symptoms that are presented. This alternative medicine is deemed safe, apart from a few instances where homeopaths have advised patients to end conventional medicine, such as vaccinations, antibiotics, but this is very rare.

I further discovered that anyone can call themselves a 'homeopath' and that there are no legal requirements as far as this area of alternative medicine is concerned. This can, of course, make it difficult to ascertain if a practitioner of homeopathy is reliable. At present, there is no single professional organisation that regulates homeopathic therapists, and whilst therapists can join many different associations, there are no laws to make it compulsory. Most reputable homeopaths do belong to, for example, the Society of Homeopaths, which is actually the largest organisation registering professional homeopaths in Europe; another one is the Council of Organisations Registering Homeopaths. In addition to this, there are five NHS homeopathic hospitals in the UK, which will care for patients suffering from a wide range of conditions, including cancer; these hospitals are located in London, Bristol, Glasgow, Tunbridge Wells, and Liverpool. The Faculty of Homeopathy is a national organisation for statutorily registered homeopaths; members are also registered healthcare professionals, such as dentists, doctors, and nurses. Before undergoing homeopathic treatments, it is advisable to ask the homeopath if they have indemnity insurance, how long they have been practicing, and if they have treated your particular condition before in others.

As for its effectiveness, according to Cancer Research UK, more than 100 clinical trials have observed how well homeopathy has worked in the treatment of a variety of conditions, including symptoms – although these trials did not provide any scientific evidence proving that this type of treatment can cure cancer, or in fact any other type of disease.

One illustration of how homeopathy is thought to work is the 'like with like' theory, and the homeopath's remedy 'Apis Mellifica', which is made from crushed honey bees and is used to treat medical problems with symptoms that are similar to the effects of a bee's sting, i.e. those that appear suddenly with a severe stinging pain and swelling. There is some evidence that homeopathic medicines work in some cases, at least.

And so, with my initial research completed and with my confidence in homeopathic medicine at an all-time low, we took steps to find a reliable practitioner, and, after a short while, we were in contact with a well-qualified lady homeopath. On the first visit, Daniel again began his running away routine; after chasing him throughout the building a few times, the homeopath locked the door, so there would be no 'escaping'. She reminded me very much of my primary school teacher from 45 years earlier, an elderly lady who wore an old-fashioned woollen skirt, had her hair done up in a bun, sported the thickest tights I had ever seen, and wore shoes that strongly resembled the older-type shoes of yesteryear.

Although she was somewhat outdated in her appearance, I guessed she was a very intelligent woman, given her bookshelves that were stacked to the limit with books – and all on the subject of homeopathy. When she took down Daniel's medical history, she again was very thorough. She asked me a number of questions regarding such things as Daniel's diet, his general health, his sleep patterns (*what* sleep?), his moods, and also his emotions. I explained to her that Daniel was unable to show emotions in any way – and that, in particular, he was unable to produce tears when he tried to cry. Just a loud high-pitched shriek was all that occurred, but that shrieking sound was far worse than a child crying. When she asked me to describe his moods, I could only really say that his moods were mostly bad and negative, which for the most part they were. This first meeting lasted for around 45 minutes, and each visit would cost £35. At the end of the first consultation, she gave me a tube of very small tablets – in fact, they were tiny – and one a day was what she recommended giving Daniel.

Each visit to the homeopath was on a par with a 'keep fit' class, as Daniel repeatedly attempted to 'escape', even with the room under lock and key. In fact, it was the door being locked that mostly added to his frustration, and confinement for him would often bring out those terrible tantrums.

A little time passed, and the pills did not appear to be working. They were changed on three different occasions, and each new remedy proved no better than the previous ones. Nevertheless, we still were prepared to give it time, and so we continued going, hoping that we would see improvements. I remember, on one particular occasion, my car was off the road due to a mechanical problem and so I asked a close friend if he would mind taking us to visit the homeopath, if I reimbursed his fuel costs. He agreed and, after the visit and on the way home, Daniel exploded for no apparent reason in this friend's car, shouting and lashing out as if something had possessed him. My friend asked how long had I been taking Daniel to the homeopath, and, when I said, 'Three months', he calmly replied back, 'Doesn't seem to be working, does it?' I was so fed up with it all, and the pills that the homeopath had given Daniel seemed to be no better than a tube of Smarties, and so on our next visit we concluded our business with the homeopath and ceased the visits. My opinion on this particular branch of alternative medicine is that I feel it has nothing to offer for individuals with brain injuries, at least according to our family's experience, and that, if it has helped others with similar disorders, I would be very surprised, but it may well have done – who knows?

Two down, and one to go; the Chinese medicine had proved ineffective, the homeopathic treatments equally so, but there was one further alternative treatment to try. After the previous two showing no positive results, would faith healing change our misgivings? I wasn't at all sure, but I once more set about researching the area.

10   Treatments: faith healing

Faith healing is a practice used by some religious groups to prevent and cure diseases, or improve an individual's health. It is done through prayer, spiritual insights, and mental practices. Faith healers claim that they are able to cure illness by divine and supernatural intervention. The actual term 'faith healing' is used by Christians who are of the opinion that God heals people through the power of the Holy Spirit, usually by the 'laying on of hands'. To rely on faith healing in preference to conventional medicine can have serious complications, though, and there have been cases where some adult patients have considered themselves 'cured' after choosing faith healing and withdrawing from conventional medicine only to die, or make worse their condition. Many Catholics hold that faith healing comes about through prayer to a saint or to a person who has the gift of healing, and the Catholic church has officially recognised 67 'miracles' and over 7,000 unexplained medical 'cures' since the Blessed Virgin Mary is said to have first appeared in Lourdes in February 1858.

There are also several recorded cases of fraud against faith healers, and one particular book titled *The faith healers* investigated some Christian evangelists, including Peter Popoff, who claims to be able to cure the sick in addition to giving them personal details about their lives, but was proved to be a hoax after it was discovered that he was receiving radio transmissions from his wife, Elizabeth, who was off stage reading information that she and her aides had collected from earlier conversations with members of the audience. In another case, at a Jack Coe revival service in Miami, Florida, Coe had told the parents of a young boy that he had healed their son, who was afflicted by polio, and asked them to remove their son's leg braces. However, the boy was not cured and this removal of the braces left the three-year-old lad in constant pain. Coe was duly arrested and charged with the practicing of medicine without a licence, although the case was eventually dismissed after a Florida Justice of the Peace threw out the case on the grounds that Florida exempts 'divine healing' from the law. Ironically, Coe was later in the year diagnosed with polio himself and died weeks later at Dallas Parkland Hospital. As the saying goes, what goes around comes around – was this 'divine intervention'?

It seems that conventional medicine is consistently the most beneficial, when compared to other treatments, but in cases when conventional medicine can offer no cure, then sometimes people will turn to alternative treatments, such as the faith healing, as a last hope – and this happens more commonly not with terminal cases, but in many other conditions. We decided to make an appointment, again with Daniel's agreement, for him to visit a faith healer. From the outset, I really did not have a lot of confidence in it helping Daniel, but we had given the other two alternatives a try, so surely it was worth this one final shot?

We arrived at the Healing Centre one Friday winter's evening at 18.00 p.m., and were greeted by an lady who appeared to be not a day younger than 80. She was a very small-framed woman whose hands, I noticed, were afflicted with arthritis. She slowly led us to a little room that contained all old-type furniture that had probably been with the old lady for many a year. The visits were free, although, as you entered the room, a box with the words 'Collections' upon it was sitting on a small shelf, situated in such a position that, to not see the box, you would have to be blind! The room itself was dark and gave off a fusty kind of smell. An old-fashioned bed with a statue of Jesus Christ on the headboard stood out against all the other items in it; the statue was made of brass, and it seemed to me that a tin of Brasso was urgently needed to restore it to its former glory. The room itself was very drab, very dull, and very depressing, and, after each visit, I was always pleased to get outside and breathe in some fresh air.

The old lady only briefly asked about Daniel's medical problems before asking him to lay on the bed. 'This was going to be a difficult task,' I thought to myself, but she then suggested I hold his hands and promise him a reward once the session was over. I used an old-fashioned bribery method: 'sweets' was the promise from me to Daniel, if he remained still throughout. Even so, I found that I had to repeatedly reinforce these words in order for them to have anything like the desired effect, and, even so, the old lady had to stop her 'healing' from time to time to allow Daniel to move about a little bit, such was his boredom.

Once the healing started, the old lady placed her hands a few centimetres from his head, and initially there was no actual contact between Daniel's skull and the healer's hands. She asked Daniel if he felt a warmth, to which he replied 'yes'. She then lowered her hands to make gentle contact with his head, and as she did so she was praying. She also asked me to pray, which I did, although scepticism and doubts were still uppermost in my mind.

And so the first session came to an end. She wrote down the name of a herbal medicine and asked that I buy some to give to Daniel. It was not a prescription, just the name of a herb scribbled down on an old piece of wastepaper. The herbal tablets had to be purchased from a local health shop and she explained to me that they might help him to sleep. In fact, these herbal pills actually did no good whatsoever, even after six weeks of a trial period; needless to say, another complete waste of money. Out of curiosity, I placed my own hands close to my head and I could also feel warmth (try it yourself), so I would suggest it's probably down to the body's own heat mechanisms. It's not just faith healers from whom heat can be felt when hands are placed very close to the head, but, I would suggest, everyone.

Our visits were every Friday evening at 18.00, and during the time we visited the faith healer, I often had conversations with a young lady who had a very seriously handicapped young boy. The boy was aged 7 years and was both physically and mentally handicapped; he was, in addition to this, both blind and without speech, and my heart felt for the young lady and her son. Week after week, we continued to attend the Healing Centre, and yet week after week no improvements were noticed. 'How long do we give it?' I wondered. A month? Two months? I decided that, after two months, enough was enough; after two months, if any improvements were to be had, then surely it would have been well within this time. The lady with the severally disabled young lad informed me that it had also not had any positive effects on her son, either, unfortunately, and so I explained that I had decided to discontinue the visits with Daniel. I added that I, at least, felt this type of 'treatment' was not a treatment, or whatever else you might call it, that could benefit people with brain injuries, and that I personally had not heard of anyone being successfully treated by these methods. It may be that it has helped with certain ailments, but, in those conditions that it has helped, would the condition have got better even without the intervention of faith healing? I will never really know the answer to that, of course, but I suspect that the conditions that did get better after faith healing would possibly have done so naturally in any event.

All the alternative medicines had been tried and all had proved to be worthless in Daniel's particular case – but it was all worth a try. And we lost nothing, but gained a lot.

11   Treatments: a visit to Lourdes

A well-known charity called the Children's Society had
become closely involved with our family after they were
informed of the difficulties that we were facing on a day-
to-day basis, in addition to our son's difficulties. They
suggested to us that he go on a pilgrimage to the holy city
of Lourdes, France, where many miracles are said to have
occurred, especially after sick people had bathed in the
holy waters. Although it seemed, at the time, a desperate
measure to allow Daniel to travel to Lourdes in search of
a 'cure', especially considering that he was not a
terminally ill boy, we knew that his condition would be a
life-long thing and, in some ways, when people are
desperate, they do tend to clutch at straws. I believe this
was so in our situation; deep inside me, I had little
confidence that simply bathing in waters could offer a
'cure', especially after the previous visits to a faith healer
had yielded no positive results, but Daniel deserved to be
given the chance to go on the trip, at least. Despite the fact
that I had little confidence in the holy waters, I knew that
simply going would be a positive experience for him. In
fact, it would without any doubt be 'an experience of a
lifetime' for him.

On the day Daniel set out for Lourdes, I felt a
loneliness that I had never experienced before in my life. I
had become so very close to my son; I spent most of the

time with him, and I adored him. I suppose my closeness to him was because of his very bad start in life, and the subsequent difficulties he was experiencing made me feel sad for him, day after day: it tugged constantly at my heart strings.

Daniel had been allocated two carers for the trip, and this made me feel a little more relaxed, but my wife and I still worried about him. Our biggest fear was that he would run away and get lost, and so I did explain to the carers that he was very good at running away, but they assured me that they would be able to run faster than him if it came to it! The trip started out from Stowmarket, Suffolk, which is a local market town roughly eight miles from our home. From Stowmarket, the coach travelled to the port of Dover, and then onwards for a 22-mile trip by ferry across the English Channel.

Most people have heard of Lourdes and the holy waters: it is a place where 'miracles' are said to occur. Millions of people, many of who are terminally ill, travel hundreds and thousands of miles to reach the site, in search of a miracle cure. It all began many years ago, on 11 February, 1858, with a young girl by the name of Bernadette Soubirous, who was a sickly 14-year-old asthmatic child raised in a religious family that had come down in the world, reduced to living in a small, miserable hovel that was formally a prison cell. It was on this day in early February that Bernadette, along with her sister and a friend, went out to an old cave known as Massabielle to collect scraps of wood. In order to reach the cave, a shallow canal had to be crossed, and Bernadette, who was worried about her asthma, stayed behind. That afternoon, she felt a warm breeze that seemed to caress her face, and then a vision manifested itself. Bernadette described it as 'a girl' who spoke in Gascon (a French dialect); the girl told her three secrets, and then directed her to dig in the cave, and hence the miraculous spring appeared. Bernadette's talkative sister quickly spread word of this encounter and crowds began to gather around the spring.

The vision of the girl that Bernadette described was, many believe, a vision of the Virgin Mary, who appeared three more times to Bernadette and also to many others. By April, a kind of hysteria had taken over Lourdes and miracles were said not to be far behind. The first was bestowed on Louis Bouriette: blind in one eye, he gathered some mud from around the spring, made a compress out of it, placed this over his blind eye, and then regained his sight. The press soon picked up on the story of Louis, and Lourdes became a very busy place. Throughout the carnival that followed, Bernadette seemed to be the only one to keep her head; she continued to have her visions and described them politely to anyone who troubled to ask. Bernadette entered a convent up north in Nevers in 1866, where she led a secluded life, always subject to ill health; she died there in 1879 at the very young age of 35. A movement for canonisation sprang up immediately and, in 1933,

Bernadette was made a saint. And as for Bernadette's role in history and religion, her own wishes sum it up: 'The less people say about me, the better,' she once said.

A statue of the Virgin Mary was erected at the site in 1864, and it is estimated that the number of people who have visited the shrine is in excess of 200 million. When Mary first apparently appeared to Bernadette, she revealed herself as the Immaculate Conception and asked that a chapel be built at the site of the vision. She then, it is further claimed, asked Bernadette to drink from a fountain in the grotto; no fountain was present until Bernadette dug and the spring emerged, and is still flowing today. The water is said to have healing powers, but science cannot find any curative properties in it that can be identified. It is alleged that many miracles have occurred at the shrine and so perhaps we must wonder if 'divine powers' are at work, or is it that a positive 'feeling of being healed' contributes to any actual healing? After all, the power of the mind can be awesome and many things can be overcome simply by having a positive attitude.

Daniel spent many days bathing in the holy waters alongside many other disabled children, and although he did not really understand the background of the site at the age he was then, we explained it all to him when he was a few years older.

The days flew swiftly by and it soon became time to pick him up. I felt quite overwhelmed that he had been given the opportunity to visit such a wonderful place, a site of such religious significance. All the lovely photos that we were given by his carers were really eye-catching, too, with the array of flowers around the statue of the Virgin Mary and the greenness of the shrubs all looking wonderful in the light of the summer. These pictures, at least, we will all treasure forever.

We did not notice any changes in Daniel at that time, but, as the years pass by, there is little doubt that he has made huge strides. He has overcome hurdles that we would never have imagined that he would be able to, and his improvements have been nothing short of 'miraculous' – but is any of this due to his bathing in the holy waters, or is it just that, as he has aged, his condition has improved naturally, or that he has become more positive in managing his symptoms? We will never know.

12   Special educational needs

As Daniel had very complex needs, our local education authority was a little concerned regarding the correct placement for our son. Specialist schools of a residential status were suggested on more than one occasion, but, as far as I was concerned, this was a no-go area, and one that I would go to any lengths to avoid. My wife and I knew that Daniel would almost certainly need to attend a specialist school, and this was a fact that we easily accepted, but we both wanted Daniel to remain at home as a part of our family unit and to be able to continue to reinforce the bond between him and the rest of the family. We were aware that many people do send their children, away at a young age, specifically for a good education, and that many children do attend the boarding-type schools, but we both knew that our son would never be a professor of maths or the like, and that what he really needed was a basic education that would assist him in getting through his everyday life. We also felt certain that, whichever schools our son did attend, there would be many problems; our concerns were not based on academic work, but his then very bad behavioural problems.

Talks after talks with those responsible for ensuring that Daniel had access to the most appropriate education in order that he might fulfil his full potential eventually concluded with my wife and I taking our son to a specialised school, recommended to us by the education representatives, to meet with the headmistress. The school was 15 miles or so from our home, and so it was within easy travelling distance for our son, and we were told that it catered for children such as him.

On arriving at the school and looking round with the headmistress, however, it quickly became obvious to my wife and I that this school was certainly not the correct placement for our son. The headmistress also very quickly confirmed this fact and, like ourselves, was amazed at how such a decision to send Daniel to her particular school had been reached. Our son, who had moderate learning difficulties, had been here referred to a school that catered for children with the severest of learning difficulties – and this first step into the education system for him made me wonder just what sort of people are in charge of making these potentially life-changing decisions? Even I, who had no prior experience of the education system, could probably have found a more appropriate placement in the first instance.

Irrespective, we continued to look around the school with the headmistress, and I felt a deep sympathy for the pupils, children who were born with such difficulties. Many were wearing helmets because, apparently, of the nature of their various conditions, which, for many, included self-harming tendencies.

Later, we left the school feeling very disappointed, but with a promise from the headmistress that she would contact the local education authority and put them in the picture as far as this incorrect placement for our son was concerned. So, back home it was, then, followed by phone call after phone call – and, as always, the person one needs to speak to is unavailable. We pestered and pestered the authorities, practically demanding that a suitable school be found for our son, and sooner rather than later.

Thankfully, after a few weeks, we were invited to another specialised school, this one ten miles from our home. When we arrived and looked around this school, we knew instantly that it was far more suitable for Daniel – although we also felt saddened as it confirmed that he would not be attending the same school as his older brother, which was only a mile or so up the road from where we lived.

Another, rather more practical concern was the fact that Daniel was still in nappies – would school staff members be willing to change him when required? If not, then this placement would be a non-starter from the offset. After discussing it with the staff, a classroom support assistant who would be supporting Daniel on the one-to-one basis agreed to change him as and when needed, and so, finally, he was now starting his first school.

The school's transport department arranged for Daniel to be picked up in a minibus, which also picked up other children; our son was allocated a one-to-one support worker to travel with him as the hyperactive aspect of his condition would not allow Daniel to remain seated for the duration of the journey, but he needed to be kept still and safe on the bus.

Three days a week were all that our son was allocated, but even three days was a huge improvement given that we had initially been told that his only option would be to attend a boarding school. The very first day that Daniel boarded the minibus was a strange occasion; he never waved goodbye or acknowledged us in any way, and he seemed a million miles away even as he first took in the surroundings of the minibus.

He was five years old when he started this school, and there were already problems, especially with Daniel's speech. The staff had great difficulty in understanding him, and much of the time he would use sign language. Daniel's behaviour was another area of concern, some of which was undoubtedly due to his not being understood verbally, which he found incredibly frustrating. Indeed, problems arose after just a few days, though, and this was the beginning of me going to the school and bringing Daniel back home. On my way to pick him up, I often wondered to myself 'will they try for a residential setting for our son?', a possibility that still gave us a great deal of concern and worry.

Also, the lady who had been employed to support Daniel on his journey to school suggested that she would soon refuse to allow him to travel in the minibus altogether, as she found it extremely difficult to contain him, and she was concerned, too, for the safety of the other children who also travelled in the minibus. We understood her concerns, of course – although, on one occasion, she actually tied Daniel to the seat, and we thought that this action was a little drastic, but perhaps it may have been resorted to in extreme circumstances.

A report from the school stated seemed similarly divided: 'Daniel's attention-seeking behaviour can be distressful to both children and staff alike and results in disappointingly poor work on occasions, but when fully concentrated Daniel is a delightful boy to work with and he can be very enthusiastic, and has made progress in many areas of the curriculum.'

The school's sports days I always found truly overwhelming, as I watched Daniel competing in all the activities. Although he won very few of the events, I always explained to him that it was not the winning that mattered, and that the achievement for him was to have participated.

Conversely, I dreaded the school discos as it was an absolute nightmare to get Daniel in the car for home at the end of the night. The discos gave him a real high, and once they had ended it was usually a case of chasing him around the school and, on occasions, up the road. It was a good thing that I had a little energy at the time – today, I would never have been able to catch him, and even back then there were times that his speed exceeded mine! When I did manage to get him into the car (with the help of half a dozen teachers), on arriving home he would hardly sleep a wink all night.

Despite that fact that I was regularly picking Daniel up from school when his behaviours were at their worst, he was making good academic progress, and, in view of this, the school's staff suggested giving him a trial period at the mainstream primary school near our home, which meant he could be at the same school as his brother, after all. But, although I too had long thought that he should be allowed a period in mainstream school, I now had reservations as I was truly concerned about his ongoing challenging behaviours. The education authority did help to lessen our concerns somewhat after they assured us that Daniel would have support, which did restore our confidence, but only marginally.

Daniel duly started at the mainstream school at the age of eight – the same school as his brother, who was ten years old, attended – but things did not go to plan and the move to this particular school soon started to go downhill. Daniel would leave the confinements of the school grounds whenever he was given the chance, and his brother, Luke, was asked by the teachers to help look after his younger sibling. I did not agree with this in any way, mainly because Luke already had a lot to put up with in the home setting without being asked to contribute to looking after Daniel at school, too – and at ten years old, it really was especially unacceptable, however you looked at it. Daniel was extremely difficult for my wife and I to manage, let alone for his ten-year-old brother.

As feared, then, Daniel's disruptive behaviours coupled with the impulsiveness of leaving the school grounds made it impossible for him to continue being taught at this particular school. Both problems are very common in children who suffer from ADHD, but the school could not manage Daniel in any way, and after numerous meetings, it was decided that he would start back at his previous school, after the half-term holidays. The teachers at the school were very understanding and really did try to help Daniel, but with other children to consider and Daniel's behaviour to contend with, they did not really have a choice.

When I was called into the school to discuss whether or not our son could continue on at the school, I knew what the verdict was going to be: Daniel could not stay on and, once the summer holidays arrived in two weeks' time, that would be his final day's attendance there. At this school, Daniel's academic work had also suffered and he learned very little, admittedly with his bad behaviour being the main barrier. On one occasion, at the school fête, a female police officer was sitting in her panda car when Daniel stuck his hand in the window and blasted the horn. He then soaked her with a water pistol, and his cheeky grin even put a smile on my face, although the police lady clearly did not really see the funny side to it all.

And so more phone calls, and back to the drawing board. 'What now?' we wondered, although the answer was perhaps was obvious as we would then ask ourselves: 'Would he be able to return to his previous school?' After making a few enquiries regarding this possibility, we were advised that a place had been kept open for him, should the need arise – perhaps those concerns that my wife and I had had about Daniel attending a mainstream school had also concerned those that suggested it in the first place? In any case, our son returned to his previous, specialised school – and to the 10-mile each way journey to the school, which was not as good as attending a primary school just up the road from where we lived, but so be it.

Daniel soon settled back in at the school, although his behaviour problems were still proving to be a barrier to his academic progress. I was, on a huge number of occasions, required to go to the school and return him back home again. His behaviour was also giving much concern again in the school minibus, and it eventually reached the stage where I was asked to take him to school directly and then pick him up again in the afternoon. As I sat in my car waiting for him in the parking area I would always observe other parents picking up their children, and watch them all walking to their cars in an orderly fashion – and then I watched Daniel being escorted to my car with a support worker holding his hand to prevent him running away. At that stage, even a simple task like walking to my car was, for Daniel, still extremely difficult. I always felt so sorry for all of the children with learning disabilities and would have loved to have been able to wave a magic wand at them and declare, 'You have no disabilities – you are now better'. But I knew this could never be; this was only the soft side of my nature taking over. Some of the children would smile at me with such innocence, and I would always think to myself, 'I hope life treats you kindly' as it always worried me how many of these youngsters might be scorned and have the 'mickey' taken out of them in this sometimes harsh world that revolves around perfection.

Daniel's academic work slowly began to improve, and eventually it reached a standard that exceeded the work of many of the other pupils at the school. The principle barrier that hampered his learning achievements improving further still remained his behaviour – and yet it was once again recommended, by the local education authority amongst others, that he be given another chance to attend a mainstream school. This concerned my wife and I very much; it had been tried before and failed, and it was unfair on Daniel for him to be continually shifted from pillar to post. He really needed a school at which he was able to settle, an established routine.

Nevertheless, the decision was taken to allow him to further fulfil his potential at the mainstream school, the one positive thing about which was that it had a unit that catered specifically for children, such as Daniel. This gave us some hope that the school might be better equipped to deal with his behavioural problems, too. It was arranged for him to be taken to school in a taxi, which was paid for by the education authority. A one-to-one carer was also required to be with him in the car for the journey to and from the school.

As soon as Daniel started the school, major problems soon followed and become commonplace. Day after day, the school rang me up to either go there and take him home, or go to the school and help to calm him down after one of his extreme temper tantrums. At other times, he would simply leave the confines of the school, and then the hunt began, with even the police searching for him. Thankfully, with so many people looking for him, he was always found – albeit some hours later. It annoyed me to some extent to think that my son was supposed to be in a reasonably safe environment and yet was able to 'escape' to outside the perimeters of the school grounds, but of course I also knew how quick and adept he could be at escaping.

It was an absolute nightmare going to the school after a phone call from the headmaster, and then watching Daniel in a rage, with anything in reach being thrown across the classroom, and everyone concerned being powerless to stop it. And as I drove home from the school with my son sitting beside me, lots of thoughts entered my head: 'Will he be taken away from us?' was still our most biggest fear, and again I would look at him sitting beside me and those wishes of neither of us existing would flood back into my mind once again.

By now, Daniel trashing items in the school became more and more common, and it reached a point where the school could no longer allow him to attend unless the local education authority supplied a one-to-one support worker to work with him. This was what I, too, had been shouting about week after week, and month after month, as we knew that our son would never be able to attend any school without such support.

Many of Daniel's frustration at that time concerned his severe speech defect; he was so unintelligible that the teachers could not understand what he was saying, and this must obviously have been very frustrating for him. My wife and I could understand some of his words, but, even with us, it was very limited. Daniel was never really offered a decent amount of speech therapy; two hours a week was insufficient, and he really needed a huge amount of therapy, but, regrettably, this never happened. After starting the middle school, a speech therapist's report summarised his progress, or lack of it, at that time: 'Phonology – this remains Daniel's greatest problem; he can make most sounds, but continues to have considerable problems sequencing sounds into words, with the result that his speech is often unintelligible. He often omits ends of words, and uses a glottal stop in the middle of words. He tries hard, but because of his poor attention span and hyperactivity, there is no long-term consistency of effort and consequently no carry-over into speech. He flits from one activity into another, and in spite of long-term speech therapy, progress has been slow and only minimal. I feel his poor attention span and hyperactivity remain a block to his future progress.' I am convinced that, had more speech therapy been in place for Daniel at the particular age he was at the time, then improvements in this area would have been much more marked.

While we were waiting for a support worker to be found, our son was meanwhile missing out again on his education. Each week, I rang to enquire if anyone had been found and for many weeks the reply was 'no', until, eventually, one call yielded good news: a support worker called Mr Dalton had been secured and was, in fact, an former teacher who had a huge amount of experience of working with children with learning difficulties. Daniel returned to the school with the Mr Dalton and things improved marginally. He began helping Daniel with much of the curriculum, and they would also undertake more practical and physical tasks, such as walks, visiting scenic places, etc., which helped with occupying Daniel's mind, as it was usually the classroom settings that he found difficult. Mr Dalton also helped our son with social issues, such as the 'stranger danger' scenario, and also with his personal habits, skills and self esteem. Obviously, he still needed to take part in the academic work, but, in doing these other activities, too, it did help to minimise his boredom, which is a common trait of ADHD.

There were still quite a few occasions when I was required to pick Daniel up from the school, but these occasions were fewer than before. In addition, his relatively calmer attitude had lessened the risk of him being excluded. When Daniel's tempers became bad at the school, though, they were still very bad: school chairs and tables would fly across the classroom as if they were peanuts, anything within reach was not exempt from either being thrown or damaged beyond repair, and all in his path was tossed aside through his phenomenal strength. Over all, though, the rough went with the smooth, and while we knew that things would never reach what we could describe as an ideal scenario, things were definitely improving.

However, it was during this time, too, that we started to become increasingly aware of the residential placements that were being suggested at the meetings I attended – and this was when worry became more worry. As long as I had breath in my body, I was determined that this would not happen. I knew that the amount of love that Daniel was receiving at home was a firm base for him to build on, and that if he were removed from this and into a residential setting, he would deteriorate.

Having settled in at this middle school for a year, the time soon came when Daniel would need to move on again and attend a high school, which would perhaps be his final move prior to leaving school altogether. Once again, the discussions began about which would be the best placement for him. Residential schools were once more suggested by the local education authority, but, as before, we were not willing to accept this option. It may have been part of the reason why it was initially difficult to find a suitable school in the first instance, but my main objection remained that Daniel's behaviour problems would still exist whichever school he attended and, with a residential school, he would not have the support of his parents and family, which he urgently required at the time. The Priory School was then recommended, which was of special status, and was 25 miles away; although it catered for children who boarded, it also accommodated day pupils, which obviously suited us all as far as that went.

I went with Daniel just before half-term to meet the teachers and to look around the school and to introduce him to the staff. I will always remember that day, walking around the school grounds with my son, and just how overwhelming I found it, what with his brother attending a mainstream school and Daniel having a very complex series of problems that would never allow him to attend the same school, as we would have preferred. It would have been a godsend for us to watch the two boys attending the same school throughout their schooldays.

Anyway, at about this time, I was informed that the support worker who had assisted Daniel at his previous school was no longer going to be employed to assist him at this new school, which were only able to offer him three days a week in any event. I did have very real concerns about our son starting this school with no one to one support him (furthermore, he was transferred without any paperwork), and voiced my concerns at the start, but the powers that be must have been under the impression that Daniel's behavioural problems had suddenly gotten better. However, it was soon to be shown to them that his problems in this area had not suddenly disappeared, and in fact were actually becoming worse.

Daniel set off for his first taxi ride to the new school, a further concern for my wife and I as he had no support in the taxi, and we were only too aware that he certainly needed someone with him in the car at all times. In the morning of the first day at the school, the phone rang, and, before I answered it, my instincts told me it was the school. I even remarked to my wife, 'Daniel needs to be picked up'. On answering the telephone came a phrase that I had heard hundreds of times before: 'Mr Collins,' the caller said, 'It's the Priory School here. We are having terrible problems with Daniel – could you please come and fetch him home?'

'I am on my way,' I replied.

On the very first day at the Priory School, Daniel had lifted a table to throw in a maths lesson, and also provoked a major playground fight. I arrived at the school to witness Daniel throwing chairs and tables across another classroom, and with one of his temper tantrums seemingly in full swing; his face reddened, his eyes bulging, he was driven by an unimaginable fury. I gradually calmed him down and, with help from the teachers, I managed to get him into the car. He always needed to be seated in the front, or he would almost certainly have tried to get out of the windows.

Each time that Daniel attended this school came the dreaded telephone calls, with hardly a single day passing without incident. I was asked to support the school in making a more measured re-integration, which I agreed to with pleasure and relief. However, after Daniel had been attending the school for a couple of weeks, a major incident occurred that resulted in me fetching him home immediately; not only did I need to fetch him home that day, but he had also been asked not to return for some time. Once the expulsion finished and Daniel returned to school, more trouble flared up; this time, it was in the taxi, with Dan constantly attempting to 'escape'. It had now reached the point where he was refused to be allowed in the taxi and I was once again required to take him to school and pick him up, which, at a 50- mile round trip, was a huge burden on our finances.

Daniel, meanwhile, had started up his old tricks and would leave the school grounds and go into town – and so the telephone calls increased.

'Mr Collins,' the caller would begin, 'Daniel has gone missing. We have called the police, who are helping in the search. Could you come to the school please?'

'On my way,' I always replied, and this was a reason I was tied up: I had to be prepared constantly for these calls, and it took over my life. I was completely restricted and not able to do many things that otherwise I would have been able to.

Time passed and then the powers that be decided to allow Daniel to travel to school again in the taxi, which to me was a huge relief. At the school, however, the problems were still continuing and, day after day, I was picking him up for home. It finally reached the point where the school would not allow him to attend until a one-to-one support worker was found, which of course meant that Daniel was missing out even more on his education. As it was, he was only allowed three days at most, and, in reality, I felt that Daniel was failed miserably by the local education authority. I had believed that every child was entitled to a full and suitable education, but this was certainly proving not to be the case for Daniel.

I asked, at one of the many meetings, why the previous helper that Daniel had been allocated could not be employed to help support him at this school? Our son was clearly not accessing a full education nor achieving his full potential, so the very least that the authorities could do was to employ a helper, as they had done before? Enough was enough, as far as my wife and I were concerned, and we could not allow this scenario to continue unresolved, so it was a case of consulting solicitors, which was more hassle, but, for our son's sake, it had to be so. Before the date set for the consultation with solicitors, though, a telephone call relayed the news that the support worker who had previously assisted Daniel was being employed to help him again. This was news that overjoyed us, and the need for a solicitor's involvement was no more.

In fairness to its headteacher, the Priory School did not give up on our son, as I am sure many schools would certainly have done considering the very difficult behaviours that he was presenting with at that time.

As the time passed by, Daniel started to make reasonably good progress and – with the help of his one-to-one support worker, the headteacher, and other members of the staff team – began to achieve many things, such as, first, numerous swimming certificates for deep-water swimming, then he passed his cycling proficiency test, and then he earned a first-aid certificate. Things had at last begun to improve, and although there were still many difficult setbacks, at least the progress he was making was another step in the right direction.

He has since become by far the best swimmer in our family, and I remember on an earlier occasion when we all went to the coast for a day, Daniel went swimming in a very rough sea, against my wishes. My wife and I were terrified watching him as he swam further and further out to sea until his head looked to be the size of a cork in the distance. It was so impressive, in fact, that a man on the beach felt moved to say to me: 'Hi, mate. I consider myself a strong swimmer, but you would certainly not get me out in those rough seas.' Almost every time we visited the coast, Daniel would run straight down into the sea, despite our telling him not to. Of course, if we could have prevented this, we most certainly would have done, especially when the seas were hostile, but we never really objected to Daniel swimming in the sea when it was calm – provided, that is, that he swam in his trunks and was not fully clothed. Needless to say, when he eventually came out of the water again, the relief my wife and I always felt was unimaginable. But his behaviour here was, again, all down to the impulsive side of his ADHD disorder; ADHD individuals tend to act first, and then think of the consequences afterwards, at least for the most part.

Of all the events and venues I attended with Daniel throughout the country, two really stick out in my mind more than the others. The first was when we went to a conference in Lincolnshire organised by a project known as Improving Choices, which helps disabled youngsters access the same opportunities as their counterparts, specifically in the realms of employment. Daniel was sitting at the front of the large hall with his tutor, Mr Jenkins, and the room was packed to full capacity. Mr Jenkins then began interviewing Daniel, with Dan answering each question in turn. The first question Mr Jenkins asked Daniel was why he was suffering from learning difficulties and ADHD, to which Daniel replied: 'I suffered from oxygen starvation when I was born.' This really did bring tears to my eyes, and I felt so very proud of Daniel. At the end of the interview, the whole room gave Daniel a standing ovation, at which point I just could not hold back the tears. I felt so extremely proud of him. A young Down's syndrome girl who was sitting next to me made me feel even more proud when she told me that she, too, had enjoyed Daniel's interview very much. She really touched my heart, and of all the positive things I have discovered in my life, chief amongst them is just how caring and loving these children are. Most do not like to witness harm to others, such is their pleasant nature.

Secondly, the sports days I attended at Daniel's latest school were similar to those that I had enjoyed at his previous schools, and always touched me. The only real difference at this school was that he actually enjoyed me coming to watch him, whereas, at his previous schools, it had seemingly made no difference to him. It was as if he had become more emotional and was able to show his emotions that much better, too.

Considering that Daniel was attending relatively short school weeks, he was nonetheless given many opportunities, such as a trip to a hostel in France with the Priory School as part of an exchange programme; he did a cycling marathon for charity with Mr Jenkins, his tutor, and two other boys; he gained work experience at a gardening organisation, called the Walled Garden, one day a week that was mainly run by people with learning disabilities; and there were many other, similar events that he also enjoyed. There were also some in which he was unable to participate, though, simply because of insufficient available support, and, at the time, he became really upset about this – and I found it extremely difficult, too, to explain to him the reasoning behind these decisions.

Although the above-mentioned cycling trip was a success, it was not without incident. For example, when the group were halfway to their destination, they decided to stop for a drink – at which point, a Post Office delivery van ran over the rear wheel of Daniel's bike. However, despite the fact that the wheel was completely buckled, he did manage to complete the run!

The time was drawing close to when Daniel would finish his school years, yet his neurological problems were still potentially a barrier to him being able to secure and hold down employment after leaving full-time education. This coupled with his interests in mechanics led to him being allowed to stay on at the Priory School for an additional year and a half; not in the main part of the school, but in a separate unit where he would be able to study further in preparation for a college course. Whilst his attendance at this time was still only between two and three days a week, a one-to-one tutor continued to support him throughout this period.

Daniel also began helping out in a small garage one morning a week, but, although he enjoyed it, the impulsive nature of his condition soon made it apparent that it was unsafe for him to continue, which was quite upsetting for all concerned, as the work had proved therapeutic for him. He was then offered a place at the local college, but unfortunately things did not go according to plan here, either, and many times we were unable to get him to attend, however hard we tried or whatever rewards we offered him. The taxi would arrive at our home to take him to the college, but Daniel started his running away act – again and again. Some mornings, he would refuse to get in the taxi, and I would take him in; at other times, he would not even travel with me. It really was a blow to my wife and I, and it resulted in Daniel giving up the course, which again was heartbreaking, especially considering how much time and effort had gone into securing him a placement in the first instance. It was as if he had lost his motivation.

13 ADHD and adolescence

The teenage years were, perhaps, the worst times of all as Daniel's hormones kicked in and added to the problems and pressures that already existed. These were the times that I would be out searching for my son, night after night, when he had failed once again to come home. Daniel began drinking alcohol, usually to excess, and it was not unusual for me to drive through the streets of our local town at night looking for him, only to come across, say, crowds of people gathering around an unconscious person in the road – and I always knew instinctively who that person laying in the road was. On one occasion, as I duly tended to my son, the sorrow was simply overwhelming. He continually banged his head on the ground, with blood spurting from open head wounds, and then the ambulance arrived, followed by the police who handcuffed him securely in order to prevent him from harming himself any further. At the hospital, the head banging continued, with security guards helping me to calm him down, and the sadness I felt in my heart for my son was unbelievable. There were many times during such incidents that I really felt like ending Daniel's life along with my own. Each and every day seemed filled with these heart-rending feelings, and, as for god, I disbelieved in any such being; if he did exist, then I hated him for allowing my son to be born with these terrible difficulties, especially those that he was facing at that time.

This was also when it was truly established to me how people with mental health problems are shunned and victimised because of their disorders, while their counterparts who suffered from many other of the common physical conditions were, it seemed to me, not. Some of the responses that were directed at our son were beyond belief. It hurt us deeply when, for example, we witnessed him covered in phlegm after other youths thought it was 'good fun' to spit body fluids over him, and to leave him crying and in a state of severe distress. It horrified me to sit with him at the hospital after another individual had repeatedly kicked him around the head, knocking him unconscious, and all for what? Simply because he had learning difficulties and was a vulnerable person, in addition to being an easy target for the alcohol-fuelled 'hard men'. It sickened me to the core when I picked him up in a severely distressed state after another young man had deliberately urinated over him in the gents' toilet of a public house, with two others blocking the doorway and preventing him from leaving. It beggars belief imagining how a human being could do such things to his fellow man, and it made me feel at times very ashamed to belong to such a species called 'man'. But then I would be reminded of all the good, decent people out there who did help our son at times when he desperately needed it.

We managed to persuade a local youth football team to let our son play in their team once a week, which was always on a Monday evening at 19.00 p.m. Week after week, though, one of the youths would constantly kick Daniel up the backside, and, although Daniel reported this to the person responsible for looking after the youngsters, it still continued. Our son became so downhearted over this that he packed the football training in.

It seems that the main reason that the perpetrator had done this to Daniel was because of what he perceived to be Daniel's 'overreaction', which is in fact simply a common facet of ADHD; ADHD youngsters are known to be sought out by people, including school bullies, simply because of the way that they 'overreact'. We always did our utmost to ensure that any individuals who assaulted our son were subject to the criminal justice system; frustratingly, though, whilst one was prosecuted (he was fined the large sum of £50 and told to 'be a good boy'), the other escaped scot free.

Most of the police officers who helped me to get Daniel back home, for example, were understanding, although I felt at times that not all of them understood the issues surrounding mental health issues. This concern is purely based on my own personal experience in my son's case, though.

Disappearing into thin air was one of Daniel's best tricks, and to just take your eyes off of him for a minute was all that it would take: his impulsiveness would strike and he would be gone, no explanation as to where, and with distance as no barrier. Then came the oft-repeated scenario of going to the police station, filling in 'missing person' forms, and then the hunt was on. On occasion, I would find him myself, but, at other times, the phone would ring and relay a message that I had heard so many times before: ' Mr Collins, we have found your son. He is unconscious and an ambulance is on its way. He will be taken to [X] hospital.'

'OK,' I always replied, 'I am on my way.' At the hospital in circumstances such as these, Daniel would often bang his head on the floor repeatedly, perhaps in sheer frustration, and as I cradled his head in my arms, I might silently pray for his release from this dreaded yet recurring situation and out of a world that did not make any sense to me, either, crouched there on the floor with my shirt and trousers covered in my son's blood, more and more hospital visitors staring at us as we became the main focus of attention. And then hospital security staff would, as ever, come to our aid and help me to prevent Daniel from further harming himself.

On some occasions, Daniel was taken to hospitals much further away, mainly because he had been in a different area when something had happened to him, and obviously he then needed to go to the hospital in that particular catchment area. A few times, he was transferred to a hospital that was nearest to a specialist head injury unit because of the nature of his injuries.

Most of the police officers locally knew Daniel, not because he had a criminal record, but because of their contact with him and our family when he went 'missing from home' or when he became intoxicated in the nearby towns. Relatively recently, though, Daniel came fairly close to receiving a criminal record when, at a nightclub, he was being provoked into a fight. The other person would not leave him alone, and he overreacted after the police were called, and would not go away when asked. I was unaware of the incident until 03.00 a.m., when, after Daniel failed to arrive home, I rang him on his mobile – but there was no answer. I knew that whenever he did not answer his phone, trouble lay in store, and so the hunt was on again, and I went out as usual searching the streets of the town. There was not a single person in sight and so, from there, it was a trip to the police station, which was unmanned but had a button you pushed in order to be connected to the main switchboard. After speaking with the policeman on the other end, he informed me that my son had been taken to another police station, many miles from the nearer station, as the nearer station was full up and busy. I made my way to this other station, and arrived at 04.30 a.m. – but I was unable to talk to my son, or even see him, until around 10 a.m., which meant that he had been held in a cell without representation for all these hours. I sat in the police station almost in tears.

'Surely, this cannot be right?' I thought to myself. 'A young man with learning difficulties being held in a cell and not even allowed to see his father?' Absolutely dreadful, and for what? A public order offence that was dealt with by way of a fixed penalty fine – after all he had not committed murder, he had not broken into a house. In my opinion, he should have been dealt with by way of the fine once he reached the police station and then released for home, but I can only imagine that it's a routine procedure, and these rules apply to all. In many ways, I can understand why some people do desperate things at times like these, and I myself felt very desperate that I was not allowed to see my son that night, but, what option had I except to sit and wait.

When Daniel was younger, things had been extremely difficult – but those were, it now seemed, the days of the calm before the storm, and now that storm had finally reached us. Relationships were a very difficult area for Daniel – not uncommon for individuals with an autistic spectrum disorder – and he had a huge amount of difficulty in comprehending relationships with females that were to be a 'friends only' basis. He always thought that girls who befriended him wanted a deeper relationship, and it was very sad to pick him up from outside of a girl's home where he would be crying and deeply distressed after he had pursued a girl or thought she was his girlfriend, when, in reality, she had simply wanted a 'friends only' relationship.

One particular incident regarding a young girl and Daniel that I will remember always was on one of those occasions that he had gone missing. I had already telephoned the police and an officer had advised me to stay at home, and that he would come out to our home, just in case Daniel contacted me. My wife and I were again, and as ever, fraught with worry. When the policeman arrived, I was still trying to contact Daniel on his mobile phone when a girl on the other end of my son's phone then answered it and explained that Daniel was stone drunk in her flat, which was approximately 15 miles or so from our home. The policeman offered to drive me there to pick him up. We had no trouble finding the location, or my son, but the flat was an upstairs flat, and the policeman and I struggled like anything to get Daniel down to the ground floor level. The occupants of the flat were known to the police, we later found out, and Daniel's new mobile phone had been stolen. The young lady repeated that she had not seen his phone – and yet she answered it earlier? We were also later told that the flat was used for the purpose of drug taking, but as far as I am aware our son was spared this horror.

We always dreaded the fairs coming to our local towns as this always spelled disaster, too. Fun fairs really fascinated Daniel – the bright lights, the rides, the music and everything else you associate with fairs – and I was unable to prevent him from going to them, but at least I could drive him there and pick him up afterwards, to prevent him from hitchhiking and so that I could be sure that at least he would arrive safely. He would never be at the arranged pick-up point, though, and so began the searching and then another trip to the police station to register my concerns. The police assisted me on numerous occasions after Daniel would not leave a fair and get in my car to come home; there were often dramatic scenes as the officers lifted him physically into my car.

As may already be obvious through earlier anecdotes, Daniel was an extremely vulnerable teenager: he would talk to anyone and could have been very easily abducted, simply because he did not realize that not all people are pleasant. He saw no bad in anyone. On one particular occasion, he was actually picked up by a pervert during one of his hitchhiking escapades – and I use the word 'pervert' as I feel it's appropriate for what this man suggested to my son, as well as the fact that his actions resulted in Daniel actually jumping out of the moving vehicle. The police were involved in searching for the culprit, but no-one was ever apprehended, possibly in part due to the fact that Daniel never gave a thought to noting down the registration number of the vehicle involved. Furthermore, even after this particular nasty incident, he continued to hitchhike if the opportunity came up, even after being reminded by the local 'bobby' of the dangers of hitchhiking.

It was also during his teenage years that Daniel discovered that he enjoyed nightclubs, as did many other youngsters of his age. Several friends said to us, 'I would not allow him to go to nightclubs', but we had to be realistic – and why should he not be allowed to go? He deserved the same opportunities as his peers, what were we supposed to do? Keep him under lock and key? No – as far as we were concerned, he should, as far as possible, be treated the same as other 18 year olds. The nurse from the community mental health team, too, advised that our son should be allowed to lead his life, and that, however much we wanted to mother him, we had to let go, to some degree. In reality, we would never have been able to physically enforce a ban anyway.

I also knew, in my heart of hearts, that Daniel going to nightclubs was going to create additional problems for us, too, and it was not long before these problems arose, with Daniel not coming home or more ambulances attending. I suspected that maybe others were deliberately getting our son intoxicated, due to the nature of alcohol's effects on him; when he's been drinking it, he became a different person, although unlike some others he was not aggressive or violent.

In any case, it was now a weekly occurrence for Daniel not to come home after the nightclub closed, even though his taxi fare was always on the table (we had to leave the taxi fare on the table, otherwise he would have certainly spent it all on alcohol). I recall, on one occasion, the time reached around 02.30 a.m. and there was still no sign of him. Generally, if he had not arrived home by this time, I would ring him on his mobile and, on the times he did not answer, I knew that some sort of problems had occurred, and so I would get dressed and drive to the local town to look for him. As ever, this would involve me driving down the main street searching and searching. This time, there was nobody in sight – only a dark figure laying on the pavement. On closer inspection, though, it soon became clear that this dark figure was Daniel, drunk out of his mind and with his face covered in his blood – a result of either hurting himself when he fell, or where person or persons unknown had assaulted him. Time for a call to 999 and yet another trip onwards to hospital. Of course I knew that Daniel was not safe on the streets; I knew that he would have been safer in a 'containing environment' – but then what a horrible thought. Again, my determination drove us both on and I reinforced my outlook with the thought that: 'one day, with enough support, Daniel will became a productive member of society'. That night, though, it was difficult to remain positive; our son would either take a downward spiral into a life of crime, stealing cars, housebreaking, and other criminal activities, as some ADHD youngsters do, or he would indeed come through it all to become a good and decent young man. The small part-time jobs that he did in the local vicinity, not only occupied his mind but were good for him in more forward-looking ways, too. He was a large boy, but as gentle as a lamb and would not harm a fly; obviously, there were a few who would try and exploit his good nature, but all in all he was well liked by most people locally who knew him then.

At 18 years old, Daniel's ultimate ambition was to ride a motorcycle, and, while my wife and I were not happy with this idea, did we have the rights to stop him? Why should he not have a small motorcycle, as many other youngsters did? He deserved to be given the same chance as them, and so we decided to let him take his CBT (compulsory basic training test), which is what all people have to do before being allowed to ride a motorcycle. The younger learner drivers go out on the road, usually two or three at the same time, with an instructor following and observing that they are safe, or as safe as can be expected at the time. The instructor then gives advice about any driving errors, dangers, etc. that the youngsters make, and, at the end of the training, the young rider is issued with a certificate stating that they have attended a CBT test course.

I had taught Daniel to ride a motorcycle on fields near to where we lived, and I felt confident that he would pass his test, which he did. To get his full licence, though, took almost a year, such were the strict regulations for people applying to drive with certain disabilities; these included medical questionnaires, doctors' reports, etc.; nevertheless he did eventually receive his provisional licence and we all were over the moon. We really preferred the idea of him driving a car, though, and so purchased a small Nissan Micra for him, which he drove, with me sitting beside him (although I found this very nerve testing), on 'L' plates. But Daniel did not want to drive the car – he still preferred a motorcycle – so, in the end, we reluctantly let him have his first bike, a small Honda 125. For a month or two, everything appeared to be going well, and some friends even commented on how a good rider he was, although this did not really make my wife and I less concerned about his safety. However, after Daniel had been riding his bike for three months, the dreaded phone call from the police: 'Mr Collins,' said the caller, 'It's the police. Daniel has been involved in an accident, and, although he is not seriously hurt, he has been taken to hospital complaining of pain in his leg.' I immediately left home to meet with the policeman at the accident spot. The officer informed me that Daniel had driven into the back of a van, which was stationery, at a set of traffic lights. When I mentioned to the policeman that my son had learning difficulties, he suggested that I persuade Daniel to surrender his licence on health grounds – and, at the time, I agreed to his request out of sheer worry for Daniel's safety, despite thinking to myself 'did he deserve another chance'? Yet, if he was killed on the roads, would we be able to live with that? Although he was a good rider, his lapses of concentration were clearly a factor in whether or not he was safe.

At the hospital, the policeman spoke to Daniel first and suggested again that he surrender his licence. Our son went absolutely berserk; this was his only means of transport and, living in the area that we did, it was in many ways his lifeline. The alternative, however, was that the police would prosecute him for driving without due care and attention and, the officer added, he would ask the court to withdraw Daniel's licence in any event, so it was a no-win situation. I then spoke with Daniel and he reluctantly agreed to hand over his licence, adding: 'I may as well be dead'. He signed the policeman's notes authorising him to take his licence away and send it to the DVLA. This was a sad situation in many ways, but a good thing in other ways: Daniel would lose his independence without his licence and, living way out in the country, the loss would be of tremendous hardship to him; yet, it gave his mother and me some peace of mind, and I certainly would rather be his taxi than see him come to any harm.

After a few months had passed, Daniel contacted the DVLA with regards to his licence and, under some section or other, they advised him that he would be getting his licence back, after all, as he met all the criteria for holding a licence, and his medical conditions in themselves were not in the criteria range under which the DVLA could withhold his licence (although careful consideration of illness and medical disorders are taken into consideration). And so, when Daniel came running out in the yard shouting, 'Dad, I am getting my licence back!', I did not know how to react, but I certainly was most surprised.

Nevertheless, Daniel is back on the road and each day we reinforce to him the importance of driving safely. If he has another accident, he may not escape so lightly, and it may result in him losing his licence for some considerable time. The other down side to it all is that he continually runs out of fuel; the phone rings and I say to myself, 'here we go again'.

All this said, though, it's still a pretty good achievement for him to have obtained his licence in the first place.

14 ADHD and family life

Our family became quite famous over the years, but for all the wrong reasons – what with a newspaper article regarding our story being published, and then a feature in one of the woman's magazines, and finally an invitation to have a talk on a local radio station, which, while I found it a little daunting, did give me the opportunity to talk candidly about just what it's like to have a family member affected by a condition such as ADHD.

As may have perhaps already been understood through our story so far, the effects of having a family member affected by ADHD can be devastating to the extreme. In many cases, 'normal' family life is disrupted big time, and this can last for many years. In fact, in some cases the effect it has on families, including siblings, can last for a lifetime. Children grow up watching their ADHD brother or sister having extreme temper tantrums, watching as items in their home are destroyed, listening to inappropriate language, listening as friends say to them 'your brother is stupid' or 'your brother is thick' and other equally hurtful comments. Parents, too, are often subject to very embarrassing situations, such as being out shopping when their child has a temper tantrum and starts using bad language, with people looking in disgust at the inappropriate behaviours. Indeed, I have witnessed this on a number of occasions, and have overheard such comments as, 'what that boy needs is a good hiding' and 'that child is out of control'. In reality, though, any child suffering with ADHD may be very difficult to control, and it's way beyond their capability to control their tempers or their inappropriate language or behaviours.

Siblings notice that their ADHD brother or sister receives a great deal of attention, and will see a host of various professionals visiting their brother or sister, which can make them feel 'left out'. This can, in some cases, lead to some sort of rebellion, and the family may find themselves with not only the ADHD child who is being difficult but with siblings who are, too. Parents of other children sometimes stop their youngsters playing or associating with the ADHD child, probably because of the challenging behaviours and the languages, or because they worry about learned behaviours from the 'naughty child'.

Siblings may also be deprived of the main thing in life that they truly needed and deserved – a sufficient amount of attention – simply because the ADHD child can, in many cases, take such a huge amount of time and effort in being looked after by their parents, who are then unable to devote the same amount of time to their other children.

Siblings of ADHD children often fall behind with their own schoolwork, and, in many cases, their teachers are unaware that the child is enduring a family life that can be far from the norm. A peaceful, happy home life for these children who have a sister or brother affected by ADHD or with similar behavioural problems can be a non starter.

A day out at the seaside or other locations is, in some cases, not such a perfect day out as it should be, and is instead filled with stress for the siblings, who may look forward to going to the seaside only to have it spoilt by either returning home early with their parents, or because their parents are unable to focus attention on them due to the fact it needs to be focused more on their ADHD brother or sister.

It may seem like an easy solution for the parents to simply remember to spend more time focusing on the siblings, but, in reality, this can be very difficult, what with constantly chasing the ADHD child, looking for them after they have disappeared for the umpteenth time, and worry, worry, and more worry. On the occasions our family have been on holiday only to return home after the second day due to an unimaginable amount of problems, it was really Daniel's siblings that suffered, of course, but as a parent of an ADHD child, you reach a point where you have no choice; you can stick it no longer, and even an hour becomes too much.

Another area in which siblings of an ADHD child can experience difficulty is in friendships, as many other parents do not like the idea of their child associating with a child who has a brother or sister who behaves inappropriately and uses bad language – which may be understandable on a parenting level, but it is very difficult for the sibling to understand why his or her friends don't come over to spend time with them.

Health is another area that can be affected by sharing family life with an ADHD individual, in that parents of ADHD children can, in some cases, suffer from a host of problems such as stress, high blood pressure, and depression; the health of siblings also can be affected in similar ways.

15 Overcoming the impossible

Daniel's housing needs are a major concern to both my wife and I. Although, in an ideal world, we would love him to stay with us until we pass on, this would not really be fair on him as he needs to learn his independent living skills in preparation for when that time comes. He finds it very difficult to manage finances and in keeping tidy and prioritising things; he still needs to learn that, when he lives independently, he must put food before alcohol, he must keep himself clean and tidy without constantly being reminded, and he must learn to budget for all necessities. We feel it will be better for him in the long term to learn all these things while we are still here; obviously, because we will be able to support him. We have been advised by professionals that this is the best way forward, and we will also try and ensure that Daniel has accommodation that is within a reasonable distance from our home.

We will always worry about our son, as we have since the day he was born, and the thought of him living independently is our present concern, but at least we feel more confident today that he will get by – it certainly would never have even been considered some years back.

Daniel has achieved many things in his life including overcoming huge odds. He has many deep-water swimming certificates, a cycling proficiency certificate, a provisional driving licence; he has made speeches at charity functions; and he has been to France twice. He has helped to raise funds for charity by doing a cycling marathon with another two lads and a tutor.

He has now overcome the requirements for any medication, including the Concerta (Ritalin) and he is, as I write this book, now in the process of being discharged from the care of the mental health team – again, this is something that we would never have dared to imagine would happen. He is also now in the process of learning to drive a car, and I feel certain that he will eventually pass his car test as he did with the motorcycle CBT test.

His speech, too, has progressed, from an unintelligible noise to an almost perfect speech tone, which is unbelievable. The severe speech defect he had for many, many years we thought would be with him throughout his life, as did many of the professional bodies involved in his care. His conquering it was certainly not down to the very limited speech therapy that he once accessed for a short time, but was done through sheer determination on his part.

Although it still might be difficult for Daniel to hold down full-time employment at the moment, this is something that we are working towards for his future. Furthermore, he already works part time, and on a fairly regular basis, for a professional couple in the adjoining village, and has been helping them with gardening work for the past three or four years. I am sure that the couple – Penny and Michael – have been an inspiration to him. Penny, I feel, keeps him in his place to a certain degree, and Daniel knows that she will put up with no nonsense, which is a good and positive thing as he must learn to abide by certain rules, the same as everyone else does.

I believe that Daniel will always have some difficulties in a few areas of his life, in addition to being 'vulnerable' to a certain degree, but I see no reason why his fantastic improvements cannot continue. After all he was once a child who was completely 'uncontrollable', he was like the very devil himself, but has since grown up into a well-mannered, well-liked and considerate man. It just goes to show that so many of these kids, with the right guidance and devotion of others, can and do overcome the impossible, as he has done. God travel with our son Daniel.

Epilogue

Attention-deficit hyperactivity disorder (ADHD) is a neurobehavioral disorder. The condition affects both boys and girls, although it is more prevalent in boys, with a ratio of between four and five boys to one girl affected. Although there are many theories, the actual cause, or causes, of ADHD remain unknown for the most part.

ADHD has been understood as a particular condition for many years, despite lacking a formal or identifying name. In 493 BCE, a condition that now seems compatible with ADHD was described by the physician and scientist Hippocrates. Centuries later, in 1845, a German physician and poet named Heinrich Hoffman wrote a book of verse about the inappropriate behaviour patterns of several children, one of which was titled 'Fidgety Philip' and was the story of a young boy who was very hyperactive. Later still, in 1902, an English paediatrician, George Frederic Still, delivered a series of lectures at the Royal College of Physicians (London) in which he described a group of children with quite severe behavioural problems. These problems, he suggested, were down to hereditary reasons rather than bad parenting, which had initially been suspected.

More recently, it has been again suggested by scientific research that there is a genetic link to ADHD, such that, in identical twins, for example, there is a very high percentile chance that if one has the ADHD disorder, then the other twin will also suffer from the condition. It is also suggested by research that 50 per cent of parents who suffer from ADHD will have a child who is also affected by the condition.

Another suspected cause is birth trauma, and, as our son suffered from a birth trauma and, consequently, ADHD, I feel that I am in a position to agree with this being cited as a probable contributing factor.

A further possible cause currently being investigated by scientists is the apparent imbalance in ADHD individuals of chemicals called dopamine and noradrenalin; both of these chemicals function as neurotransmitters and are known to assist in regulating attention and activity. Research suggests that the parts of the brain that are affected in ADHD individuals are the basal ganglia and caudate nucleus, the cerebellum, and the frontal lobes, which seems likely as these are areas of the brain concerned with behaviour.

It has also been documented that women who smoke and drink alcohol whilst pregnant increase their risk of having a baby with ADHD. Whether or not this is the case, I can't say as I actually have known women who did smoke and drink throughout their pregnancy, perhaps before the risks of doing so were truly known, and none of their offspring are affected with the condition. Perhaps it is simply that the risks are small in this case, or that it is only one of several contributing factors? Nevertheless, commonsense should prevail: it is not advisable to drink or smoke during pregnancy as other hazards may be enhanced, in addition to risk of ADHD, which may be of harm to the baby at birth or indeed in later life.

Levels of lead, even very low levels, in the blood of pre-school children is also thought to increase the risk of suffering with the disorder. In this day and age, lead is of course not allowed to be used in paint substances (as it was some years back), so, again, it would seem that the risks from lead must be minimal?

Diet, too, has been suspected of causing ADHD, but no studies to date have been able to fully support this theory. Restrictions on certain foodstuffs, such as sugars and sweeteners, made no apparent difference to ADHD children when removed from their diet, and although, in some children, certain foods may make a child more active, it is not a lasting scenario as it is with ADHD. We have tried the elimination diet on our son, but it had no benefits in relation to his condition.

Specifically, some people believe that additives – such as the 'E number' and colouring tartrazine used in some drinks – cause ADHD, but, again, this has not yet been proven. Such additives may contribute to the symptoms, but they do not seem to actually cause the disorder. Nor does caffeine cause ADHD, contrary to popular belief.

As already mentioned, molecular genetic research has shown that there may be a possible genetic link behind ADHD. Occasionally, though, the disorder has instead been speculated to be down to poor parenting skills, with the parents blamed for their child's behaviour, but it has been established beyond doubt that this is not the case. Sadly, parents do nonetheless blame themselves. ADHD is a disorder that affects all classes of people, from rich to poor and is prevalent in most countries where studies have been undertaken. Whether a child has a good education or otherwise, the disorder can affects anyone.

There are other conditions that commonly accompany ADHD, such as a learning disability, and the research I have undertaken in this area suggests that between 20 and 30 per cent of ADHD children will have an emotional disorder, which, in turn, will have an effect on their behaviour.

Oppositional defiant disorder (ODD) can in some cases co-exist with ADHD; about 50 per cent of ADHD children will have also present with this condition, mainly boys. With ODD, the child can be more aggressive in a physical way, tempers may be worse, and defiance and stubbornness may also be noticed.

Another condition, called 'conduct disorder', can accompany ADHD, too. This may be more serious as it can, and does in some cases, lead to conflict with the police, through stealing, carrying weapons, housebreaking, committing acts of vandalism, being cruel, and so on. Figures are sketchy as to the ratio, but it is estimated that between 25 and 40 per cent of children with ADHD will also have a conduct disorder.

A small percentage of ADHD children will also have Tourette's syndrome. This condition manifests itself by twitching of the face, involuntary movements, blurting out words, and tics. It can be helped by medication.

Bipolar disorder is another condition that can co-exist with ADHD, but only in a very small number of cases. With this condition, friendships are difficult to establish, or, if friendships are established, they tend to last for only short periods. Children with this disorder are extremely sensitive to failure and rejection. The stimulant drugs that help ADHD children can actually worsen the mania for bipolar sufferers.

Some children who suffer from ADHD are known to also succumb to depression, and, even into adulthood, this depression can continue.

Another poignant fact about the ADHD disorder is that many sufferers have a low self esteem; they do not think highly of themselves, they feel 'worthless and down in the dumps', and this is one of the reasons that the disorder needs to be diagnosed and treated as soon as possible, as understanding that there is a reason for what they are feeling and experiencing may help many to achieve more in school, and help with any anxieties that they may have.

There are a number of symptoms and characteristics of ADHD, including the following:

- inability to follow instructions;

- attention seeking behaviours;

- finding it difficult to remain seated;

- restlessness;

- talking loudly and talking a lot;

- impulsive behaviour patterns;

- difficulty in getting to sleep;

- having extreme amounts of energy;

- disruptiveness;

- easily distracted from tasks given;

- early sexual maturity and sex drive (boys);

- takes risks;

- tendency to interrupt others' conversations;

- easily led;

- not being able to pay attention;

- temper tantrums, from minor to extreme;

- destructiveness;

- poor social skills;

- difficulty in making eye contact;

- likes to flitter from one activity to another;

- clumsiness;

- challenging behaviours, and;

- short-term memory loss.

Although all of these symptoms may not be occurring, there is a strong possibility that many will. Some children with ADHD present with only a couple or so of these symptoms, whilst in others the majority of these characteristics may be discernable.

As indicated in earlier chapters, the most common type of treatment prescribed for ADHD children (over six years of age) are stimulants, a group of medication that includes methylphenidate, which is specifically known as Ritalin or Equasym (both tablets) and Concerta (capsules).

The specific treatment will depend on the individual, though, and medication is not suitable for all children; however, it is known to benefit the majority of ADHD individuals. Other drugs associated with ADHD include dextroamphetamine, which may have the brand name 'Dexedrine', and which can be used in a lower age-range group (3 years and above). It Dexamphetamine is a stimulant, but is known to be quite effective in controlling hyperactive behaviours in some ADHD individuals.

Atomoxetine ('Strattera') is a non-stimulant medication used in the treatment of ADHD. It works in a different way than the stimulants, and increases a chemical in the brain called noradrenalin, recorded as being effective with respect to the impulsive nature of ADHD. It is also known to increase the concentration span.

Estimates of how many children who suffer with ADHD go on to have the condition as adults are said to be between 60 and 70 per cent – but my instincts and experience tell me that this figure should be higher. Suffice it to say that the majority of children who suffer from ADHD will still have the condition into adolescence and adulthood. In fact, in many cases, they will continue to have the disorder for the entirety of their lifetime, although, on reaching adulthood, many will have learned to control the symptoms much better.

Also, many adults with ADHD have never been diagnosed as having it, yet will have endured the condition's associated difficulties throughout their lives, such as holding down employment, keeping appointment times, difficulties in getting organised, or getting up and dressed and ready for work. These are everyday tasks that people tend to take for granted, and yet for the ADHD individual these tasks can be really challenging. The main reason that these ADHD adults were not diagnosed as children is that they were simply regarded as 'naughty children' – and, for many of these who were not diagnosed and treated, the outlook is less positive than for those that were correctly diagnosed. Either way, adults with ADHD can still be hyperactive, but not as severely as that experienced in childhood; adult ADHD sufferers tend to feel restless and fidgety, and relaxing can be difficult for them.

Relationships for adult ADHD sufferers are another difficult area, and marriages may well have been irretrievably broken down. Substance abuse, including the excessive use of alcohol, cigarettes, or drugs, is suggested to be higher amongst ADHD adults than their non-ADHD counterparts. For adults who have the condition, it is preferred by most to have employment that offers activity, as sitting down all day is a difficult task for most of them and is a no go area; this is why many ADHD individuals flitter from one job to another and find it difficult to hold down jobs where as they are not active. ADHD persons can also find it difficult to manage their finances, and, as a result, can often find themselves in debt. It's often a case of not getting their priorities right; for example, they might buy cigarettes and alcohol as opposed to paying for the important things, such as the rent or utilities bills.

It has also been suggested that ADHD in women can be more of a challenge than in their male counterparts. Certainly, women with the condition are less likely to be diagnosed with ADHD than males with the condition. Female ADHD sufferers are not usually as hyperactive as their male counterparts, and many are not diagnosed with the condition until later in life; some not being diagnosed until they are in their forties, if at all, and it is often only as a result of their children being diagnosed that they are lead to the diagnosis in themselves. It is also suggested in some research that women are at a higher risk of suffering with depression than males who have the disorder.

Furthermore, regarding non-diagnosis or an ignorance of the condition, a sad fact is that some ADHD adults are dismissed as lazy, clumsy, hyperactive, idiots, and so on. The probable reason behind such misunderstandings and criticisms is that it is a difficult condition to fully understand, and, again, if a person has never had close relationships with an affected person, then it is without doubt a difficult thing to fully comprehend.

The diagnosis of ADHD in an adult is reached after a thorough evaluation assessing, for example, how long the symptoms have been noticed, which usually will have been from a very young age (5–8 years old); other criteria that will be looked at include an individual's employment history, social skills (including social functioning), any leisure activities enjoyed, friendships, driving history (including accidents), what their behaviour was like in childhood, whether there is any history of substance abuse, or if the individual has a criminal record.

Treatment for adults with the disorder will vary from person to person, but will include medication, sometimes in co-existence with anti-depressants if required, therapy to help with any behavioural problems, and psychotherapy treatment. The latter helps the ADHD individual with any emotional difficulties that they are experiencing; it may be in the form of visiting a psychiatrist on a regular basis, or other professionals, or group therapy could be offered. The most common medications used for treating adults with ADHD are the same as with affected children, i.e. stimulants. Adults with the condition may also benefit from anti-depressants, particularly if they suffer from mood swings and anxiety problems.

The actual symptoms in adults and children are very similar, but with adults the hyperactive component may be less severe as the adult is better able to deal with it. Adults with ADHD can also suffer from low self esteem, lack of social skills, impulsiveness, underachievement, bad time keeping, difficulties in resting, poor organisation skills, poor short-term memory, feelings of frustration, loss of concentration, and finding it difficult to stick to routines.

According to one report that I was reading recently, people who suffer from other mental disorders in addition to ADHD may also suffer discrimination from friends, family, and, in some cases, health professionals. It is estimated that one person in four will at some point in their lives suffer from some form of mental illness. The Mental Health Foundation concludes that action must be taken to deal with the stigma in our society surrounding mental illness.

⁓

I always consider myself extremely honoured to have a son like Daniel. He has given me far more than I can ever give to him, and he has made me a better person in many ways. Before Daniel came along, I had no idea of ADHD, nor of the impact that such a condition has on family life. Because Daniel is part of our lives, I have had the great pleasure of delving into the world of many other remarkable individuals, including barristers, psychiatrists, psychologists, neurologists, mental health workers, and many, many more. I have visited locations that otherwise I would never have had the privilege so to do. Because of Daniel, I have written books that in different circumstances would surely have been a non starter, as writing books would have been the last thing on my mind, and it has actually encouraged me to continue.

Daniel has also made me realise that many disabled children are enormously gifted, and that what they lack in some areas of their lives they certainly make up for in other areas. Each and every child is unique, and I have met with a large number of these youngsters over the years and have been really surprised at the achievements of many of them.

You have read, in this book, of all the negative behaviours that Daniel has succumbed to, but there have also been many good times when his behaviours are dormant, and, during these times, he is a wonderful person. Our youngest son will always have some problems in certain areas of his life, but, as time continues to pass us all by, hopefully these problems will become fewer and less severe. He has quite recently been withdrawn entirely from medication and, at the time of writing this book, his tempers are once again slowly beginning to worsen – but we will ride the storm and hope that he can manage to cease taking the medication on a permanent basis. Only time will tell.

On a final note, it must be borne in mind that not all ADHD youngsters suffer from the types of behaviours that Daniel was affected by, and that some such children are hyperactive but will never suffer from such extreme challenging behaviours.